MURDER, NEW ENGLAND

ALSO BY M. WILLIAM PHELPS

The Devil's Right Hand:
The Tragic Story of the Colt Family Curse

The Devil's Rooming House:
The True Story of America's Deadliest Female Serial Killer

Perfect Poison

Lethal Guardian

Every Move You Make

Sleep in Heavenly Peace

Murder in the Heartland

Because You Loved Me

If Looks Could Kill

I'll Be Watching You

Deadly Secrets

Cruel Death

Death Trap

Kill For Me

Failures of the Presidents (co-author)

Nathan Hale: The Life and Death of America's First Spy

Love Her to Death

Too Young to Kill

Never See Them Again

Kiss of the She-Devil

And don't forget to check your local listings and watch
M. William Phelps on his Investigation Discovery (ID)
channel show, *Dark Minds,* in which he sets out to solve some of
the country's most notorious unsolved serial killer cases using a
very special guest star, "13," a convicted serial killer!

Murder, New England

A Historical Collection of Killer True-Crime Tales

M. William Phelps

Award-winning, national best-selling author, star of the
Investigation Discovery channel show *Dark Minds*

LYONS PRESS
Guilford, Connecticut
An imprint of Globe Pequot Press

Lyons Press is an imprint of Globe Pequot Press.

Text design: Sheryl Kober
Project editor: Kristen Mellitt
Layout artist: Mary Ballachino

Library of Congress Cataloging-in-Publication Data

Phelps, M. William.
 Murder, New England : a historical collection of killer true-crime
tales / M. William Phelps.
    p. cm.
 ISBN 978-0-7627-7843-0
1. Murder—New England—History. 2. Crime—New England—History. I.
Title.
 HV6533.N22P44 2012
 364.152'30974—dc23

                                                    2012015239

Printed in the United States of America

10 9 8 7 6 5 4 3 2 1

TABLE OF CONTENTS

Introduction

Ralph Waldo Emerson believed emphatically in what one writer called the "mystical unity of nature and the divine." Leader of the transcendentalist movement, Emerson, at one time a minister, espoused the idea that everything we become is rooted in the environment we create for ourselves and the spiritual awareness we cultivate throughout our lifetimes. Living and writing in the specific environment of New England, Emerson believed, gave him a broader sense of a greater philosophical truth. "Nature magically suits a man to his fortunes, by making them the fruit of his character," the memorable pragmatist once ruminated.

Much of Emerson's thinking and writing was influenced by the miraculous surroundings (*his* observation, not mine) he encountered in and around his hometown of Concord, Massachusetts. Emerson adored New England and everything it had to offer. Not just plant and animal life, either. Strength in community, in addition to raising a family and the benefits this rewarding task projected out into the world, combined with the idea that *every* human being plays a vital role in society, graced Emerson's work and fostered his popular campaign of self-awareness. Emerson, in other words, was promoting the same ideas behind the modern-day philosophy of *The Secret*, 150 years before Rhonda Byrne turned it into an international phenomenon and mega-bestseller. You want the real "secret," well, read Emerson's "Self-Reliance" essay.*

Emerson and transcendentalism aside, New England has always been known for its charming tranquility and picturesque landscapes, and for its great wealth of respected, renowned, and award-winning poets and writers. (Today, it's also known for its confrontational rivalry between Red Sox and Yankees fans.) There

---

* A quick Internet search will turn up a downloadable version of this remarkable essay.

are beautiful town greens scattered throughout the six states making up the Northeast—New Hampshire, Vermont, Maine, Connecticut, Massachusetts, and Rhode Island—along with beautiful wooden gazebos of every type. There are bed and breakfasts and SETTLED IN . . . signs tacked to the fronts of creaky clapboard homes built during the eighteenth century or before. Everywhere you look, this corner of the country is painted in ribbons of rolling green hills, farm fields, fresh produce stands, and apple orchards. There is history —American Indian, Revolutionary War, and Puritan—under every rock, in every town. Beaches along the shores of Maine, Massachusetts (including Cape Cod and the islands), Rhode Island, a small portion of New Hampshire, and Connecticut have garnered welcomed and deserved praise from visitors worldwide. Movie stars own property along these same shores. The Kennedys have called New England home for generations. Presidents vacation in Maine and on Martha's Vineyard. It is no secret, in fact, that we in the Northeast take pride in our culture, our land, our history, our clam *chowdah;* and don't realize (or give two shakes) that we pronounce over as *ovah,* or car as *cah,* and say things like, *What a wicked pissah.* There are a wide variety of museums, science centers, wineries, antique shops, historic homes, nature trails, rivers, streams, mom-and-pop penny candy stores, lakes and reservoirs, even several casinos, not to mention scores of maple syrup farmers. We claim Nathan Hale and Jonathan Trumbull as our own; Mark Twain and Harriet Beecher Stowe; Katharine Hepburn and Martha Stewart. Just about anywhere you turn in good ol' New England, you walk on historic, sacred ground, with echoes of splendor beckoning your attention and respect. You haven't lived, some here will argue over pints of Sam Adams ale, unless you've experienced Mother Nature's wrath during an old-fashioned Nor'easter.

Yet there is another side to this peaceful, perhaps rustic and pastoral image, small-town and Norman Rockwellian (a man who called

Massachusetts home) as it is—a much darker, more menacingly evil, violent and, yes, even intriguing, aspect of New England life.

All the murders we've had.

Murder is the taking of one human life by another—or, as in some of the cases you'll read in this collection of New England murder stories, both contemporary and historical, *several* lives. Lizzie Borden, so goes the legend, killed her parents here (although she was acquitted of the crime). New England has also produced the likes of the Boston Strangler, British au pair Louise "the nanny killer" Woodward, more recently Philip "the Craigslist Killer" Markoff, and Pamela Smart, that devious, super-sexualized New Hampshire school teacher who seduced two students into murdering her husband. And these are only a few of the infamous murderers to which we in New England are forced to stake claim.

Lucky us.

I have spent my career writing books about murderers and serial killers, with my focus primarily on females who kill. I have written five books set in New England, two of which are about female serial killers. People are sometimes shocked to hear the particulars of these two cases: that a rather innocuous, seemingly nonthreatening female in her thirties, a blonde bombshell who drove a minivan full of kids around historic Northampton, Massachusetts, held down a respectable job, volunteered at the local homeless shelter, ran the Secret Santa program, and came across as an all-around "good" person, could kill, by some estimates, one hundred men; or that in another case, a Bible-toting caretaker, also in her thirties, a woman who donated to the local church and seemed to be the sweetest little thing, adored by the Windsor, Connecticut, town in which she lived, could have murdered forty-four people, including both her husbands!

But it happened. And both cases occurred in small New England communities where the price of corn and tobacco, budget cuts, and PTA gossip were what residents talked about at the local service station, diner, after church, and the grimy watering hole more than anything else. These were conversations shockingly interrupted by the news of how two serial killers preyed on innocent men and women, killing sometimes with other people in the same room—and for years nobody suspected a damn thing.

One of the dynamics I require in all the stories I cover is that there be a bucolic sentimentality and setting to the case—some sort of an "I cannot believe this happened here" reaction to the crime by the community. We see this more and more, it appears, today. Or maybe the reporting of this phenomenon has grown. Who knows? But turn on the news and you're apt to hear the story of some young mother "driven by demons" to put her kids out of their misery, drowning them and then laying them out like dolls on the floor before calling the cops to turn herself in; or maybe a couple of lowlife, career criminals who decide to bust into a house and, after raping the kids and mother in front of the husband, set them all on fire; or a son who feels as though his time is better off spent playing PlayStation and smoking weed all day instead of working for a living finally decides, *What the hell, I think I'll bludgeon mom and dad to death and drain their bank accounts;* or maybe a daughter, plagued by abuse all her life, puts one between Dad's temples while he sleeps (and perhaps some of us cheer for her). In one case, the son of a well-to-do stockbroker took an axe to Mom and Dad as they slept one night—an axe, for crying out loud. This college boy viciously thumped his own mother and father, repeatedly thrusting a steel axe into their bodies and skulls! Dad died after bleeding profusely all over the house while searching in the dark for a telephone to call 911. Mom lived (though she was grotesquely maimed and disfigured for life), only to identify her son to the police as the attacker, and then—get this!—turn around and stand by him in court, proclaiming she'd gotten it all wrong.

These are the cases we hear about during the evening news, shriek, and ask, *How the hell did that happen here—in the quiet, charming elegance of good ol' New England?*

None of these cases is included in this anthology; I mention them only because they show us how wide a spectrum murder can encompass, and how the least likely culprit is generally the one you should be looking at first. You are more likely to be murdered, in point of fact, by someone you know rather than a stranger.

Still, looking at all these cases might also cause one to consider: *Why do these stories interest us so much?* Additionally, *Why is New England—the suburbs, particularly—the ideal setting for a collection of true-crime murder cases?*

The short answer is that murder in exurbia is much more compelling and darkly romantic—even gothic—and more rare than murder in a big city, which is, in the larger cities throughout New England (Boston, Hartford, Bridgeport, Manchester [New Hampshire], Providence), sadly enough, a common occurrence to which we don't pay as much attention as we should. Within some of the small towns throughout New England—Gloucester, Canton, Westerly, Portsmouth, Ogunquit, Goshen—where you'd think fishing and antiquing and gardening and fair-hopping are the traditions we love and most adore (and we do), lie several examples of how murder, for the rich or poor, educated or not, can find you if you've become the unlikely target of a psychopath. Doesn't matter where you live, the type of vehicle you drive, or how much money you have in the bank. Your race makes no difference. Neither do your religious beliefs, social status, or political views. If someone—and ninety-nine times out of a hundred, I will say this again, we are talking about a close family friend, sibling, husband, wife, relative, or neighbor—wants you dead, he or she will find a way to get the job done. And there's nothing, effectively, that you can do to plan for or stop it.

But please don't be alarmed by my pointing out the evils of society; the odds against your being a victim of murder here in beautiful New England, as in the rest of the country, are so astronomical that you'd have a better chance at winning one of New England's many lottery games and hedging your bets for a multi-million-dollar payday!

In this collection of New England murder stories, I tried to focus on those cases that spoke to the customary strengths, interests, and even failures experienced here in New England. I wanted to show by example how murder is something that tears communities apart and, shockingly, throughout a four-hundred-year period (1600 to 2000), how murder has always been committed for the same reasons, and in some cases in the same ways. For example, in the following collection you'll read about a gentleman in 1879 who lost his job and had it out with his boss, walked home, and killed his three children. Then there's the 1673 case of a woman who was burned alive by (apparently) her son. There's a business deal between two men that went horribly bad and ended with one man killing the other in a fit of rage. There's the sadly true tale of a young man outside Boston who, set to inherit his great-grandmother's fortune, couldn't wait until the old lady passed away naturally.

And those are just a few.

You see, the murders committed today are no different—psychologically speaking—from those committed four or five hundred years ago. People generally kill for the same three reasons: love, money, or revenge, with various branches of motives (jealousy, for example, falling under the "love" heading) protruding off those three. Motives have not changed since the Bible's Cain and Abel, and they will carry on until the end of time. What's interesting about this particular collection is the setting and manner in which each victim—and, in some cases, multiple victims—was murdered, the aftermath, and the community's reaction to each crime.

I grew up here, in a working-class neighborhood just east of Hartford, the state capital of Connecticut. I have traveled all over the Northeast on book tours, vacations, and visits with friends and family. The burning question I get more than any other is: *Why do people kill?* The answer to this is rather trite, certainly not what the person asking the question is looking for or wants to hear, for that matter. It's not the quixotic, sound-bite quote you're apt to hear by some crime-expert talking head on Nancy Grace or any other cable TV crime show.

The truth of the matter is that most murderers don't know themselves why they kill; they are acting out a primordial urge (or even instinct) some claim is beyond their control. Killers who later talk about their crimes in an honest manner mention an inherent struggle raging inside them between moral good and moral evil, the dark side ultimately and eventually winning most of the time. Serial killer of women and children Tommy Lynn Sells once said that his first kill released an explosion of anger inside of him. From that crime on, every murder he committed—"chasing the dragon," as he put it—failed to produce that same high, yet he kept on killing anyway.

Killers fight this moral battle alone, without mentioning the turmoil to anyone, thus refusing to get the psychological help they obviously need. There is, for some, a feeling of shame—not to be confused with empathy—or lack of remorse that seems to override all other emotion or practical, material thinking. Of course, there are clinical factors involved, too: the sociopath, the psychopath, and so on. For the most part, there is generally no rhyme or reason as to why one person crosses that line and kills. Some believe every human being is capable and can be driven to kill under the right circumstances. I would encourage those who think they could not be driven or convinced to commit a murder to read Patricia Highsmith's sharply disturbing novel *Strangers on a Train,* and put yourself in the position of Highsmith's character Guy, asking this question again as you read.

As Dr. Jonathon Pincus states in his excellent book, *Base Instincts: What Makes Killers Kill?,* "Crimes like serial murder and murder-for-profit mostly seem to be inspired by evil, not illness." In other words, there is a psychopath at work in these cases, catering to a sociopathic gene and abusive upbringing. He or she is killing for the sake of feeding an inherent desire to curtail, or calm, the evil rising to the surface. I see this time and again in the many different serial killer cases I have investigated over the years. A killer chooses a certain type of victim and, like a leopard in the wild, begins to prey upon this person and kill for the sport of killing. The high, if you will, is in the hunt and the kill. I would add crimes against children and women to Pincus's astute analysis, also. It's almost as if these types of murders are committed by people who cannot help themselves or stop what they are doing. Serial murder definitely falls in the realm of addiction. Serial murderers don't seem to weigh in on whether what they are doing is right or wrong, nor do they care. It needs to be done. Period. It makes them feel good. I once spoke to a serial killer who had raped and killed women in the most vile ways imaginable, but spoke about the crimes as if he were describing washing his car or taking out the garbage. His chilling words of evil were uttered with the calm, professional demeanor of a professor discussing his class's subject.

Dr. Pincus also talks about how an "internal pressure based in mental illness" generally pushes killers over the edge and to the point of taking another life. He mentions how brain damage can lead a person down a road that eventually involves murder. So, the motivating and mitigating factors, the answers to that question of *why* someone kills—emotionally, clinically, and maybe spiritually, too—are far and wide, a vast sea of possibilities. Part of the problem with studying this dark aspect of human nature is that after being caught most killers will lie when speaking about their crimes, either to minimize their role and feel better about themselves, justify the crime, or enhance the notoriety of their crimes in order to take more credit than they should—i.e., the hubristic killer.

When we step back in time, as a few of the stories in the following collection will prove, we see an epidemic of household heads killing family members. It seems that throughout the late 1800s, men killed their immediate family members (wives, sons, and daughters) more often than today. Looking at this, you have to wonder why. Why do people kill their siblings and/or spouses, sons, and daughters? Remember Andrea Yates? She's that strange-looking woman in Texas who chased her five children throughout the house one afternoon while her NASA engineer husband was at work and methodically drowned them in the family bathtub, only to call 911 and report her crime afterward. Yates is a sick person, suffering clinical depression, self-loathing, and a host of additional psychiatric ailments. Those types of killers believe that the future for their children is so bleak that only death will save them from the pain. Why else, you'd have to wonder, would a man (or woman), faced with failures at work and in his social life, deeply depressed, already leading a solitary existence, take it out on his own children? Instead of facing the fact that life has its ups and downs, why do some choose to kill their family instead of allowing them to face the future? I hope to explore some of the answers to these questions in the pages that follow.

For certain, there's something for every crime fan in this collection: history, Mafia, infamous murderers (female and male), and just about every type of murder imaginable. The sorrowful fact is that every story is true, and real victims lie at the hearts of these cases. To those from centuries ago all the way to today, I want to extend my sympathies to the families of these murder victims, both living and deceased. Genuine people like those we brush shoulders with every day were viciously murdered. And within that heartbreaking reality, beyond the pain of loss, lies the true burden murderers place on society: When and where will they strike next?

CHAPTER 1

The Strange Death of Rebecca Cornell

February 1673: Aquidneck Island,
Narragansett Bay, Rhode Island

FEBRUARY 12, 1673, WAS A COLD NIGHT, RATHER GLOOMY, THE earthen ground outside Rebecca Cornell's home hard as rock, soil frozen a foot deep at least. The seventy-three-year-old woman had been buried days before—but word around Portsmouth, Rhode Island, a neighboring Newport borough, was that the old lady had been murdered and now she was coming back from the grave to haunt the living.

On this frosty evening, Rebecca's brother, sixty-four-year-old John Briggs, was having trouble sleeping. Tossing and turning, Briggs could not get comfortable. There's no doubt the thought of his sister being burned to death weighed heavily on Briggs's mournful heart and mind. But something else, Briggs would later explain, happened in the room where he lay, just four days after Rebecca had died so tragically. It was an incident, in fact, that by the end of the week would spark one of the most intriguing and bizarre murder investigations New England has ever known.

Somewhere "between sleeping and waking," Briggs later said, he "thought" he felt "something heave up the bedclothes twice." It was such a profound sensation that it startled him awake. There was someone, Briggs felt, in the room with him. He was certain of it.

Now Briggs was entirely awake—sitting up, looking around the room. Just a silver of bright light from the winter moon protruded sharply through the darkness, cutting the blackness in the room like a door left ajar with a candle burning outside in the hallway.

Who goes there?

Briggs could sense a presence in the air. He never said whether he believed in the supernatural, or if he considered ghosts and goblins mere hogwash; but John Briggs described this event in an open courtroom as though it were fact and not a soul in that room listening had yet questioned the authenticity.

Collecting himself, Briggs rubbed his eyes. Then a light, he recalled, "like to the dawning of ye day," suddenly lit up the entire room. His hands in front of him, same as the wall on the opposite side of the room, became as clear as if the sun shone through the window.

Not quite believing his eyes, Briggs could now see his way around the room.

And there she was, he claimed, standing bedside, looking down at him.

"A woman," Briggs reported. She just stood there at first. He was certain of what he saw. The woman's attendance "much affrighted" him, he later testified.

"In the name of God, what art thou?" Briggs asked of the woman in his shaking voice.

The woman, shaking, staring at Briggs, "cried out," he said, stating clearly: "I am your sister, Cornell. See how I was burnt with fire."

Briggs looked closely at what he later referred to as an "apparition." The woman was "very much burnt," he reported, "about the shoulders, face, and head."

"I am your sister, Cornell," she said again. "See how I was burnt with fire."

And then, without a sound, she was gone.

For John Briggs, this visit by his sister was not only a sign, but evidence. Rebecca Cornell had not died in an *accidental* fire, as the town and her family had assumed since her death days before. John Briggs was now certain: Rebecca had been murdered.

Even more bizarre than John Briggs's middle-of-the-night vision, especially when considering modern-day courtroom standards, was what happened after Briggs went to the general attorney, John Easton, with this story of the supernatural vision he had witnessed in the middle of the night.

Briggs's statement "reopened the investigation into the death of Rebecca Cornell" and initiated the trial of a man no one at first believed could have been responsible for what was now considered a heinous and diabolical *series* of monstrous crimes.

After Briggs brought his information to the general attorney, the town was forced to ponder the question: If Rebecca Cornell, a wealthy Aquidneck Island society widow, who mixed it up on occasion with some of Portsmouth's and Newport's most influential and important people, had been murdered, who was it that killed the woman? And, maybe more important later as a surprise suspect emerged, why?

Rebecca Cornell owned one hundred acres just over the Newport town line in Portsmouth, on the western side of Aquidneck Island. The Cornell homestead was located on the water, a magnificent piece of property, with breathtaking sunset and beach views only those lucky enough to afford it could enjoy. She lived in a two-story home equivalent to seventeenth-century New England standards, very specific to early Rhode Island architecture. New England homes of the era had a distinctive quality and look about them, especially out on the islands off the shores of Rhode Island and

Connecticut. Many were clapboard, with large, spacious rooms in which families could gather and entertain one another, read the Bible, sew, or just sit and talk. Cornell's home had small, glass windowpanes (twelve frames over twelve frames). One writer claimed Cornell's house, in particular, was equipped with "six windows across the second floor east side [and] five across the first (because of the front door)." The home was big enough for Rebecca, her son Thomas, her grandson Edward, Thomas's wife Sarah, and a few stray boarders, one of whom was a man named Henry Straite. There were other children, Thomas and Sarah's two daughters, along with John Briggs, Rebecca's brother. A big family by any standard, but Rebecca didn't seem to mind allowing them to stay in the home, provided everyone pitched in and did his or her share of the chores and helped with the household finances, food, linen for clothing, and medicines.

One of the main fixtures of an early New England home was the often immense and centrally located fireplace, with its red-brick or garden stone chimney jutting upward through the center of the roof. It was a central attraction inside the home during winter months where families gathered, kept warm, talked or knitted, read, had tea and cakes, or just rubbed their hands together and cuddled up next to the crackling fire. The women sewed in rocking chairs with heavy blankets covering the lower halves of their bodies. They sometimes cooked breads and pies and jams in the hearth. The men smoked pipes and chit-chatted. The fireplace was the focal point. As Elaine Crane wrote in her book about the Cornell case, *Killed Strangely*, "[I]t is certain that the most dramatic feature of Rebecca's first-floor chamber would have been the large walk-in fireplace."

Think big, like a pantry. This fireplace heated the entire downstairs, although it's a good bet that every room in the house (as in most homes) was fortified with its own fireplace, however big or small.

Rebecca slept on the first floor, and on the afternoon of her death, February 8, 1673, she wasn't feeling well. Lately, Rebecca was spending more of her time in her room. The conditions under which her co-inhabitants all lived had not turned out the way Rebecca had envisioned when she allowed Thomas and his large family to move in. There was tension between Thomas and Rebecca. They were always at odds. Rebecca had every reason to be mad at her son. In fact, she had been telling friends and neighbors that Thomas and Sarah had all but abused her regularly. Rebecca shared one story in which she alleged "neglect" on the part of Thomas and Sarah. Rebecca had gone out to collect firewood (a chore, mind you, she should not have been doing to begin with, given her age and health) when she slipped on the snow and ice and fell. She lay there, on her back, struggling. Thomas and Sarah had seen it happen, Rebecca was certain; but neither had reached out a hand to help.

Another problem Rebecca had with Thomas, however, stemmed from money she believed Thomas owed her. The agreement Thomas had made with his mother consisted of his paying what Thomas later described as "six pound a yeare, & Diet for a maide servant." Thomas had already owed his mother one hundred pounds when he moved in, a debt he had promised to pay. Yet he "refused to pay" the six pounds rent or hire maid services "unless she forgave him the hundred pounds." They had been at an impasse: Rebecca refusing to forgive the debt, Thomas not willing to pay her. Moreover, Thomas wouldn't lift a hand to tend to the pigs or help Rebecca in the garden during spring and summer, nor would he allow Sarah to help his mother with the cleaning of the house. Essentially, Rebecca, who had lived a long life by the standards of the day, was left to do everything herself. What's more, Rebecca complained to neighbors of having to sleep on certain nights without blankets during the winter. She even said Thomas and Sarah would not "allow her" to eat with the family.

Because of the way she was being treated, Rebecca often talked of killing herself to neighbors and friends. She just couldn't take it anymore. Yet every time that evil thought crept up on her, a God-fearing woman, Rebecca found herself denying it, thinking, *Resist ye Devil . . . resist ye Devil. This too shall pass.*

There came a time that winter when Rebecca had decided enough was enough. She had told her other son she wanted to move in with him and his family. She wanted to leave Thomas and Sarah without anything. They did not deserve it. Rebecca was adamant when talking about moving. It couldn't come soon enough, she said not long before her death, adding the foretelling caveat: "If [I] am not otherwise disposed of, or made away."

Thomas walked into the Cornell house on February 8, 1673, and was told that Rebecca had not been feeling well that day. The sun had just set. It was near dinnertime. A cold snap had taken over the home, even with the fire in the main chamber burning.

After Thomas got himself settled, he went into Rebecca's room. She was lying in bed. Thomas's son, Edward, was there by her side, too, keeping his grandmother company.

"[I] came into the room and sat down," Thomas later testified. "[We] discoursed . . . for ye space of about one hour and a half."

Finished speaking with his mother, Thomas claimed, he went into the room next door for reasons he did not later talk about. Thomas spent about forty-five minutes alone in that room (his and Sarah's bedroom), according to later testimony by Sarah, winding "a quill of yarne."

Rebecca wasn't eating large meals these days. On that night, the family was sitting down to a meal of "salt-mackrill." It was a dish, Rebecca often complained, that "made her dry," and she absolutely despised it. In place of the briny fish, Rebecca often requested a bowl of warm milk. There was some indication that maybe Rebecca didn't have all of her teeth, and that milk and soft foods were the only nutrition she could get down without complication. Still, near 7:00 p.m., Sarah fetched Edward and told him to go into Rebecca's room and find out if she wanted her milk. The rest of the family was preparing to sit down at the dinner table and eat.

Edward obliged.

They were all sitting in the dining room as Edward got up, excused himself, and walked into his grandmother's chamber.

"Grandmother, grandmother," Edward said as he sauntered into the room.

A moment later, however, Edward ran out of the room, excited and shouting about something he had seen that frightened him dearly.

There was "some fire in the room upon the floor," Thomas later recalled, "and the child came unto us [to] fetch the candle to see what fire it was."

Rebecca's boarder, Henry Straite, had just come in from being gone all day, along with another boarder, James Moills, and both "went presently into the room" to see what the commotion was about. Thomas, Sarah, and the others followed.

In an awkward mishmash of words, Thomas later recalled what happened next, saying, "Henry Straite coming in saw some fire and stooped, and with his hands raked fire upon the floor, supposing it to be an Indian that was drunk and burnt, so he layed [sic] hold of the arm, myself immediately following, [and] by the light perceived it was my mother."

Henry Straite's account backed up Thomas's.

Thomas cried out, "Oh, Lord . . . it is my mother."

Rebecca Cornell was the burned corpse in front of them. It was not some drunken Indian who had sneaked into the home (a strange remark, it would seem at first blush, but one must understand that the Cornells had had a problem with Indians breaking into the home).

Rebecca was all but unrecognizable. She was burned and blackened to a crisp, literally. James Moills later talked about what he saw upon entering the room, shedding a bit of light on how badly Rebecca Cornell had been burned, but also begging the question: How could this woman have been burned in this manner while her family began to eat dinner in an adjacent room? How could a fire rage so wildly as to burn a human being—a task that takes sustained temperatures upwards of about 2,000 degrees Fahrenheit—and not ignite the remainder of the wooden house? Not to mention that the curtains and valances and foot of Rebecca's bed were also burned up and yet, Moills explained, "ye fire about ye bedstead was out."

"Rebecca Cornell [was] lying on ye floor," Moills reported, "with fire about her, from her lower parts near to ye armpits."

Moills had only recognized the burned-up human being as Rebecca "by her shoes."

A coroner's inquest was held immediately inside Rebecca's house. A heavy snow came down that Sunday morning, February 9, 1673, when William Baulston, Portsmouth's coroner, a very good friend to Rebecca's deceased husband, "impaneled a twelve-man inquest panel." Some of these same men had been summoned to Rebecca's house the previous night as word spread throughout the community that she had died mysteriously and suddenly in a fire. Now they were back that morning to make a swift judgment regarding her death. With the evidence left behind, it would be derelict to assume Rebecca had died in an accidental fire. Some of Rebecca's clothing was burned while some was not. She was found on the floor on her left side. What's more, the fire seemed to be contained to her body alone, with very little of the room burned. Ruling out spontaneous human combustion (which certainly did not exist as a scientific cause of death then), one would expect at least a few hard questions to be asked as these men studied the scene.

But William Baulston did not feel Rebecca's death was anything more than an absolute and dreadful "accident."

"Clothes very much burnt by fire," Baulston observed, "and her body very much scorched and burnt by fire." Baulston recorded that after a "diligent inquire," in which he interviewed all of the witnesses inside the home that night and studied the body after stripping its clothing, Rebecca Cornell was "brought to her untimely death by an Unhappie Accident of fire as she sat in her [room]."

Rebecca's body was prepared for burial later that night, February 9. The custom of the day mandated that the women perform a short ritual and clean up the body as best they could. Absent from this posse of quasi-undertakers was Sarah, Rebecca's daughter-in-law. Sarah was pregnant, and it was thought a "dead body could spirit away the fetus," wrote Elaine Crane, "or that contact could result in some deformity or birthmark." So she stepped back from helping.

Rebecca Cornell was then buried next to her husband in the family plot close along the shoreline of Narragansett Bay.

Then came John Briggs's hazy "apparition" three nights later, as he explained that Rebecca's spirit had come to him and talked about "how I was burnt," without accusing any one particular person. This vision, along with a bit of blood later found protruding from Rebecca's nose during a second inquest, along with an injury to her stomach that could not have come from the fire (but had possibly resulted from a fall off the side of the bed—no one really knew), was enough to send the coroner back to the drawing board to rethink this mysterious death.

"Briggs's account," Elaine Crane wrote, "had to be taken seriously because ghosts were taken seriously in 1673."

The theory of an accident had seemed plenty plausible before the ghost story emerged. Rebecca, like a lot of women of her day, smoked a pipe, often before bedtime. It is certainly possible that an ember from that pipe popped and ignited her clothing, or the bed (part of which *was* burned). Nonetheless, no one asked about a pipe being recovered at the scene, or the notion that for Rebecca to have been burned to death in that manner, there would have to have been an inferno confined specifically to one room in the house, or the fat cells of her body had somehow caught fire!

The coroner requested Rebecca's body be exhumed. Upon performing a second autopsy, the coroner later claimed that Rebecca had been stabbed in the abdomen—that injury to her stomach, apparently—and *then* burned to death.

Thomas Cornell asserted that it had to have been Rebecca's pipe that had started the fire. He had no explanation for the wound. As the coroner began to re-question friends and neighbors, a great animosity between a mother and her son emerged from those interviews, and it was now believed that Thomas Cornell had murdered his mother.

Thomas was then arrested and put on trial.

The court proceedings lasted one day. The showstopper was John Briggs's story of his apparition. Once a finger had been pointed at Thomas Cornell, it was hard to convince this seventeenth-century crowd of jurors, fearful Satan was working within anyone who showed the slightest bit of instability, otherwise.

Thomas was indicted and found guilty on May 12, 1673—and sentenced to death by hanging eleven days later, May 23.

"He died," Edward Field wrote in his study of Rhode Island plantations in 1902, "making no confession."

Before he was hanged, Thomas Cornell petitioned to be buried next to his mother as an indication, many presumed, of his innocence. He was denied that request and instead was buried on the same property (nowhere near Rebecca) "within twenty feet of the common road and that the Colony be at liberty to set a monument on his grave, the interment otherwise to be under or near the gallows."

Between the time of his sentence and his death by hanging, under the more severe and strict laws of the day, Thomas Cornell was bound and kept manacled by chains in his small, four-by-eight, dirty and disease-infested jail cell.

Some believe Thomas Cornell was unjustly tried and executed.

An interesting genealogical aside to this strange but true New England "murder" story is that infamous axe murderer Lizzie Borden (who was acquitted of murder!) was descended from Thomas Cornell's daughter, who had been born several months after Thomas's execution. The name Sarah Cornell gave to Thomas's child?

Innocent Cornell.

CHAPTER 2

William Beadle: Husband, Father, Killer

November 1782: Wethersfield, Connecticut

THE NOTE WAS STUNNING, ALL AT ONCE, IN ITS CLARITY AND effect. He had been their family physician for years and not a murmur of unease ever came from the family. But this disturbing letter was alarming, to say the least, and shocking in its revelations. It was William Beadle's maidservant who had brought the note, authored by Beadle, to the doctor, encouraging him to read it immediately. The maid did not know what to do. She was afraid to go farther into the house after finding the missive on the dining room table when she walked in to begin her work for the day.

"What of this dreadful purpose?" the maid queried as the doctor slid on his eyeglasses and leaned into the note to have a closer look.

"What is it, woman?" he asked. The maid was overly excited. Nervous. Her eyes undoubtedly darted from side to side, a gaze deeply unsettling. The words on the page in the doctor's hand had shattered her.

The doctor's expression after reading the note said it all: They needed to get over to the Beadle residence at once. If the note was even somewhat true, there was a tragedy inside the spacious seventeenth-century Wethersfield, Connecticut, home that William Beadle shared with his wife and four children. A tragedy on a scale the good doctor could not fathom.

"Let us first locate Esquire Mitchell," the doctor said as they started walking speedily toward Beadle's house. Mitchell was the town lawyer and one of Beadle's best friends. He would know what to do.

When the three of them arrived at Beadle's front door, all was eerily quiet. There was a sense of dread and darkness to the place, not because it was mid-December and the air outside was bitter and chilling to the bone; but the Beadle home—so often an elegant place of energetic children laughing and playing, Mrs. Beadle doing her chores, and Mr. Beadle working outdoors or doing bookwork for his trade business inside his home office— was quiet and still, as though no one was home.

They stood in front of the door, wondering who would walk in first.

Perhaps out of fear of what was beyond the threshold, the doctor, after consulting with the lawyer, told the maidservant she needed to go into the home and find out if the contents of Beadle's note actually portrayed the reality behind the four walls of this home. Neither the doctor nor the lawyer was going in.

The maidservant reluctantly walked in—what cowards these men were!—slowly creeping toward the stairs like a burglar, looking from side to side. This house, which she knew as if it were her own, was now an unfamiliar place that contained, if what she had read was really true, an unimaginable horror the likes of which no one in Wethersfield—or the state of Connecticut—had ever seen or experienced.

"With trembling hands," Mitchell later wrote about this moment, the maidservant crept quietly and shakily up the stairs, her feet and hands quivering as much from the cold as from fear and the expected scene ahead of her. When she arrived topside, she went first to the children's chamber and creaked the door open by hand, slow and steady.

What she saw was so intensely violent, "her horror so great," the maidservant "fainted and fell down the stairs backward," tumbling like a rag doll.

By now the doctor and lawyer had walked into the home and stood speechless as they watched the maid fall down the stairs.

The doctor, acting quickly, managed to catch the maid and thwart any major injuries.

According to what Stephen Mitchell later wrote, the maid "recovered her senses" while in the arms of the doctor there at the bottom of the stairs, "but [the image of that] horror stopped her utterance." She had a hard time speaking after what she had just witnessed.

Mitchell ran out of the house. There was no way he was going to confront the terrifying tragedy unfolding before them. The doctor and the maid followed quickly behind.

There were two workmen fidgeting around nearby and Mitchell yelled out to the men. He was leaning against a fence because he found it very hard even to stand on his own two feet.

"Can you men go see what the dreadful spectacle could be [up those stairs]?" Mitchell asked the men.

They looked at each other.

"We'll follow you up there," one finally said.

And so they trooped up the stairs, all three, while the doctor and maid waited.

Mitchell wrote about this moment in graphic detail, stating, "Surely a more distressing sight never agonized the human feelings than now presented itself. . . . What lay before them was clearly an act of horror no man could have done. It was so disturbing to see these children in such a state of mangled flesh."

"The floor was swimming in blood," Mitchell added.

The three men ran toward Mr. and Mrs. Beadle's room. There lay "another corpse." It was butchered too violently to identify at a quick glance.

Female, yes. Mrs. Beadle . . . maybe.

Mr. William Beadle?

Definitely not.

They soon walked down the stairs and into the kitchen. The worst-case scenario was an obvious reality once they looked down at the floor. Mitchell spelled out the feeling in the house at that moment: "Such a tragical scene filled every mind with the deepest distress. Nature recoiled and was on the rack with distorting passions."

William Beadle's letter, every last word of it, had been true.

❧ ❧

Beadle was feeling particularly depressed leading up to the day when he wrote what was now the only explanation left for what he had done to his family. Beadle had composed copious amounts of notes and letters, honest and complicated, as the months went by and he saw no other way out of a terrible situation he thought he had found himself and his family facing during what was the last year of the Revolutionary War. It was late 1782 when Beadle wrote, "I am in such a situation that I cannot procure food, raim't nor fuel for myself and my family. Is it not time to die?"

Such random death thoughts running through Beadle's mind would later be viewed as evil and twisted, as Beadle contemplated not only ending his life, but that of his young wife, Lydia, just thirty-two, and their four children, Ansell, eleven, Elizabeth, ten, Lydia, eight, and Mary, just six years old.

"But as it is a father's duty," Beadle went on to write, "to provide for his flock, I choose to consign them over to better hands."

Better hands? What did Beadle mean by that?

"How I shall really perform the task I have undertaken I know not till the morn arrives," he continued, "but I believe I shall not do it as deliberately and steadily as I would go to supper or to bed."

As Beadle wrote through his tormented feelings of despair, he spoke of how long he had been thinking about killing his family.

"Three years in contemplation," he wrote. "For I was determined not to hasten the matter, but kept hoping that still providence would turn up something to prevent it if the intent was wrong."

And so, as November gave way to December, fifty-two-year-old William Beadle, a failed businessman, shopkeeper, and merchant, had made the ultimate evil decision to kill his family. The questions running through his mind now, however, became not how he would go about this terrible deed, but when the best time would be to perform such a dark and gruesome duty.

The town of Wethersfield was not known for its association with mass murder, and certainly not filicide, during the late 1700s. Slaves loading ships ported in Wethersfield Cove were more along the lines of what one might associate with downtown Old Wethersfield (as it is called even today) back in its heyday of violating human rights and treating people like animals. Beyond that there may have been a gentlemanly clash at the local saloon, a duel, an argument that had gotten out of hand aboard a schooner docked in the cove, or some other altercation that was easily contained. Yet, as the night of December 11, 1782, progressed toward morning, this perfect New England scene, straight from a snow globe, a suburb of the state's capital city, Hartford, was about to undergo an image makeover—in a disturbingly bloody way.

From all outward appearances, William Beadle was your typical colonial man. A Wethersfield merchant by trade, he had donated monies for the relief of Boston and what the Tea Party had accomplished before Bunker Hill exploded into a hail of cannon fire and bloodshed, and the War for Independence began. Beadle knew what it would mean for business had Connecticut ports been closed to trade by the British Parliament. Beadle had been one of Wethersfield's wealthiest and most respected residents at one time; he relied on the Cove, a subsidiary of the Connecticut River (a main waterway of commerce and trade) to make his money, as did many in Wethersfield and surrounding towns. In exchange for the goods Beadle sold, however, during the early years of the war, he had begun to accept Continental currency; and it just so happened that as the war progressed over the years, beginning back in 1775, the bottom had fallen out of that money, and some were calling it worthless.

"[D]uring the Revolutionary War," Karen Halttunen wrote in *Murder Most Foul: The Killer and the American Gothic Imagination,* "Beadle's acceptance of Continental currency plunged him into economic distress, which he proudly tried to conceal from his neighbors behind a façade of prosperity."

Beadle was embarrassed by his decision. He felt ridiculed. He couldn't face up to the failure he had become. Through no fault of his own, William Beadle had lost just about everything he had worked for. He was broke.

The Beadles lived along the edge of the Cove on Hartford Avenue, in the middle of Wethersfield. William thought of himself as a society man, at home in a world in which the way you spoke, where you lived, the clothes you wore, and where you came from set the tone of your life; people judged you by the language you used, the pedigree your name whispered, and even the way in which you signed that all-important name. William was born in England somewhere near 1730 and, historian Nora Howard tells us, "apparently had a childhood of narrow circumstances, but some education." He "quoted Shakespeare with ease," Howard added, and had an "elegant signature."

This seemed to set William Beadle apart from your average Tory, peasant farmer, colonist, or Connecticut Yankee. Beadle came, as they say, from good stock—or at least he carried himself in such a manner. That close friend of William Beadle in town, Stephen Mitchell, later said Beadle never talked about "these subjects . . . I could never induce him to mention," Mitchell wrote (in his biography, *Narrative of the Life of William Beadle of Wethersfield, Connecticut: The Particulars of the Horrid Massacre*), "a single syllable relating to his age, parentage, or early occupation."

To ask Beadle directly would have been, as Mitchell put it, "rude."

Mitchell believed Beadle had been raised in or around London, somewhere near Essex. From an early age, William Beadle was said to have wanted to be a merchant, which meant one of many different things. For the most part, Beadle was your typical eighteenth-century trader. He bought goods from one person and sold them to another for a modest profit: commodities such as silk, tea, chocolate, cloth, chintzes, coffee, spices, bow strings, shovels, tools of all types, pewter, glass, liquor (rum, wine, and brandy, mainly), molasses, sugar, whale bone, paint, and several additional items favorable to where he lived at any given time.

From England, Beadle moved to Barbados, where he spent a better part of his teen years and early twenties and thirties. Shortly after turning forty, Beadle sailed off to the colonies and hit the shores of pre-Revolutionary War Colonial America a new man, looking for fresh experiences. Yet he had a hunger—maybe a hubristic, narcissistic need—for becoming wealthy and admired.

The colonies were high on the energy generated by the English for trade and tax. Contrary to what some believe—at least in Connecticut and large sections of Massachusetts—there were scores of colonists who supported England and her tough standards of living. Many did not want to stand tall and fight the mother country; they were happy being told what to do and how much to pay for a "priority" of doing business, and were rather satisfied with the strict laws England had established in the colonies.

Beadle ended up in Fairfield, a Connecticut shoreline town; and by 1773, just as word around the state buzzed that war was inevitable, he was set up in Wethersfield, a port town close to the state capital, quite advantageous to Beadle's business practices and desire to strike it rich.

Mitchell reported that Beadle owned "twelve-hundred pounds of property" (its value), which would have been fairly significant in Wethersfield. People looked at Beadle as some sort of worldly man who had money and a family born of wealth.

"His business was that of retailing," Mitchell wrote.

The one lesson Beadle had learned throughout his years of trading was not to give out credit, based on the idea that one might, at some point, eat the cost of a tremendous amount of goods a customer could not end up affording. As the war swept through Connecticut, Beadle opened a store in Wethersfield and seemed to be making solid profits, selling and trading. This windfall, however, became Beadle's downfall as he went against his own policy and began to extend credit to certain people. As soon as the dollar crashed, Beadle was left holding stacks of promissory notes for goods he had given away.

Poverty was something Beadle had written about, and talked about with friends at length, and it was clear to anyone who knew Beadle that this man had a fear of failure unlike many; and that failure to William Beadle was viewed as being worse than death itself. In a strongly worded reflection on this topic, entirely opening up himself and his feelings on the matter, Beadle ruminated:

> *If a man who has once lived well, done well, and meant well, falls by unavoidable accident into poverty, and then submits to be laughed at, depleted and tramped on by a set of mean wretches, as far below him as the moon is below the sun, I say, if such a man submits, he must become meaner than meanness itself: and I sincerely wish he might have ten years added to his natural life to punish him for his folly.*

Indeed, any type of letdown for this man was a blow to his ego and pride. He could not live to face up to it. In Beadle's skewed way of viewing life, the only way of dealing with what was a common occurrence in eighteenth-century New England was to bury your head in the sand. After all, very few lived above what might be considered a poverty level and, surely, being poor and destitute was a practice many understood as a means of survival—with the exception of William Beadle, that is. If he failed, Beadle gave up all of his self-esteem and self-worth.

Not only for himself, but his immediate family members, too.

On the night before William Beadle decided to execute a ghastly plan that would become known as William Beadle's "nefarious purpose" (coined by Stephen Mitchell, the one man closest to Beadle at the time), the depressed and insane merchant prepared a bountiful meal for Lydia and the children. He was in good spirits that night, November 18, 1782. There was no indication, in fact, that he was thinking evil thoughts. Or planning to commit a crime so heinous, it would outrage a community to the point that it would demand from Beadle eternal indemnity, reparations or compensation for his crimes for the rest of time.

Oysters. Beadle chose oysters as the family's last meal. The tone as they shucked and ate was jovial and rambunctious. And the family—along with the maidservant—sat together and stuffed themselves "very plentiful," the man of the household wrote as he envisioned slaughtering each one them like pigs.

"I have prepared a noble supper of oysters," Beadle wrote in his journal, detailing this night, "that my flock and I may eat and drink together, thank God . . . and die!"

When dinner ended, Beadle pulled the maidservant aside and spoke to her privately, whispering urgently, "You must do this errand for me"—he handed her what Mitchell called "an insignificant letter" Beadle had written—and then explained that she should not return that night after delivering the letter, that her services were not needed until the following morning.

But the maidservant did return, thus postponing William Beadle's implementation of his evil plan on this night in November.

"[It] disconcerted him," Mitchell explained, "and prevented him for that time."

On the following morning, Beadle brought his prized pistol to the gunsmith for repair, which Mitchell asserted might have been another reason why he chose not to carry out his plan on November 18. In any event, on December 10, 1782, a night Mitchell would later refer to as the "dreadful catastrophe," Beadle put into motion his plan once again, as he made the decision to end the madness going on inside his head and, with a methodic, sadistic, strange sense of repose, kill his family.

Beadle was with a group of people at his home on December 10. According to Mitchell, who did not say if he was there or not, "[H]e appeared as cheerful and serene as usual; he attended to the affairs, as if nothing uncommon was in contemplation."

His guests left by 9:00 p.m.—as Beadle begged them to stick around longer.

"Whether [Beadle] slept that night is uncertain."

One would guess he did not.

The maid retired with the children in one bedchamber, while Mrs. Beadle slept in another chamber down the hall, the same room where William would have cozied up next to his bride had he decided to retire for the night. As the evening progressed and everyone slept soundly, Beadle moseyed quietly down the hall toward the children's bedchamber, where he awoke the maidservant and told her to remain quiet and follow him out of the chamber without waking the little ones.

Beadle led her down the stairs and into the kitchen. He then explained that he wanted her to get dressed immediately, take the note he had written (he handed it to her), and walk it over to the local doctor, who lived approximately a quarter-mile away.

"Mrs. Beadle has been ill all night," William explained, handing the maidservant the letter. The maid presumed the sealed missive was a direct order for the doctor to come at once and tend to the sick woman.

"You stay there," Beadle said with authority, "until the doctor is ready to come. Do you understand me?"

Preparing for the cold by slipping on her bonnet and a thick quilt draped over her shoulders, the maidservant nodded an understanding of her orders and readied herself to leave.

"This [direct instruction] he repeated sundry times with a degree of ardor," the maid later reported.

Beadle was a man who had routinely carried an axe and carving knife to bed with him, for whatever reason; and there's a strong belief among many (including me, these hundreds of years later) that Beadle had already slit the throat of his wife before waking the maid and conversing with her downstairs.

After the maid left, Beadle walked back up that same set of stairs, entered the chamber where his children slept and, with that axe he had slept with, struck a violent, smashing blow to the right side of the tiny head of each of his four children as they lay sleeping and dreaming. With each child dazed bloodily, his or her skull busted open, the pain of which would have been the worst a human being could imagine, William Beadle took that carving knife he treasured so much and, as his good friend Stephen Mitchell later reported in tersely worded graphic detail, "cut their throats from ear to ear."

William Beadle had just murdered his four children in a most ferocious, gruesome, painful, and cold manner.

What Beadle did next would later seem bizarre and pathological, even for a psychopath. So that the male child would not soil his bed linens (Beadle was worried about what people would think when they came upon the crime scene), Beadle pulled the boy's head and upper torso so they fell over the side of the bed. This way the child could bleed out on the floor and not on the blankets or quilts.

Then, Mitchell described simply, "The three daughters were taken from their beds and laid upon the floor side by side, like three lambs, before their throats were cut."

The father of these children slit each of their tiny throats as if they were livestock.

Beadle then walked into his bedchamber and dragged his wife into the children's room, before placing her there by the children's side. He then covered each child with a blanket and Mrs. Beadle's face with a handkerchief.*

---

* This is common practice in such cases, even today. In dealing with filicide cases throughout my career, studying some of the more high-profile cases on record, it is clear to me that many of the mothers (maybe more than fathers—but fathers, too) seem to clean up after the crime and then try to make the scene as pretty as possible. They might place the child's favorite blanket over his or her body, clean and press the child's clothing, mop up excessive amounts of blood, or position the body in a peaceful (if that is even possible) manner. Some believe this indicates, without the murderer coming out and admitting it, that there is a touch of remorse, a bit of empathy there, present at the end of the crime. But the truth of the matter is, the parent feels not for the child, but his or her own self, and what he or she has lost by committing the crime.

No one knows for sure, but Beadle must have stared at them for a short time before walking down the stairs, leaving a trail of his bloody footprints along the wooden steps. He carried the axe and the knife with him and set the knife (covered with the blood of his family) on the kitchen table before sitting down "in a Windsor chair" beside it.

William Beadle then took the pistol he'd just had repaired the previous month and another he had inside the house and placed them on the table in front of him. He picked them up, one in each hand. The knife in front of him on the table was a backup if the pistols failed.

No one could know what this maniac was thinking at this point, but after taking the lives of his four children and wife, William Beadle "fixed the muzzles of the pistols into his two ears" and, without a second thought, "fired them at the same instant," blowing his head into a mash of tissue and bone and cartilage all over the wooden kitchen floor, his own lap and the dining table in front of him.

In the kitchen of the Beadle household sat a headless man, blood everywhere, brain tissue dripping down onto the wooden floor in droplets, and the remainder of the Beadle family laid out in eerie repose upstairs ("swimming in their blood and their faces white as mountain snow") for the doctor, the maidservant, and Stephen Mitchell to find.

❧

December 12. A cold morning, shaded gray. Clouds packed with wallops of snow moved and swirled in the sky, preparing to dump a winter blitz of the white powder on the state of Connecticut. As word of what was being described as a "tragic scene" spread throughout town, Mitchell wrote, "a rage" among Wethersfield residents built steadily.

The scene was so gruesome, the order of Beadle's crimes so heartless and harsh, the town took on a sense of what Mitchell described as "pity for a lady and her innocent babes, who were the hapless victims of the brutal, studied cruelty of a husband and father, in whose embraces they expected to find security, melted every heart—shocking effects of pride and false notions about religion."

It was soon discovered (and bull-horned about town) that Beadle was a deist, "and gloried in it." Beadle believed in a Maker, in other words, although he also believed that his god had tossed the world out into the universe like jacks and allowed things to happen without intervening. The omnipresent clockmaker—that was Beadle's god, a watchman who created the world and let her spin on her own. Whatever happened, happened.

By the end of that first day, December 12, the crowd gathered at Beadle's home "demanded the body of the murderer," Mitchell wrote. There was no way, this unruly mob decided, that Beadle was going to be buried with his family. The guy was a coward and a charlatan and a Devil. "Many proposed that [Beadle's body] should be [placed] in an ignominious manner, where four roads met, without any coffin or insignia of respect, and perforated by a flake."

The argument became where. No one in town wanted this wretched man's body near his home for fear that its demonic spirit might haunt them.

Finally, after much discussion, the town agreed to place the body of William Beadle "on the bank of the [Connecticut] River, between high and low water mark."

Just after that decision had been made, several went into the house and "handed" Beadle's body out the nearest window. From there, an angry posse "bound" Beadle's body "with cords on a sled, with the clothes on as it was ground, and the bloody knife tied on his breast, without coffin or box."

A horse was brought in and attached to the sled. The group got behind, as the horse pulled the sled with Beadle's body around the town, "sometimes running full speed …."

They mocked him. Spat upon him. Made angry slurs against him. All this while a horse tore about willy-nilly, bumping Beadle's corpse like a child's rag doll tied to a string.

Arriving at the river's edge some time after the mocking concluded, the group untied Beadle and pushed him down a slight hill, where his body rolled and soon found a large hole in the ground and fell inside.

For the next few days, Beadle's body was taken and put on display in various places around town for townspeople to make fun of one more time and ridicule. Kids got hold of it for a time and damaged the corpse by kicking and poking it with sticks. Then someone took the body and "removed it to a place where it hoped mankind will have no further vexation with it."

Beadle's wife and kids were interred on December 13 under a pious ceremony near the local churchyard. During the sermon given by a local preacher who buried the family, it was learned that William Beadle had been ruminating about killing his family for three years. One of Beadle's letters was read. In this striking missive, he talked about his determination and steadfast approach to killing his family, writing quite chillingly, "Any man that undertake a great affair, and at the same time thinks, ought to be very deliberate indeed; and think and reflect again and again." Beadle went on to say that on December 6, a week or so before he actually committed the murders, he had systemically and obsessively watched his wife and children sleep. And it was there, on that night, when he asked "my God whether it was right or not now to strike; but no answer came, nor believe ever does to a man on earth. I then examined myself, there was neither fear, trembling, nor horror about me. I then went into a chamber next to that, to look at myself in the glass;

but I could discover no alteration in my countenance or feelings: this is true as God reigns, but for further trial I yet postponed it."

Beadle went on to write that he had lost his faith in the Christian religion, something he had "firmly believed in for many years. . . . When I consider men as Christians, I look at them as free agents; I have examined both old and new testaments, and must think that is either their true meaning and intent—but when I consider man as a Deist, or one that does not believe in revelation, I think him a perfect machine, and that he can do nothing, but as he is operated upon by some superior power. I have renounced all popular religions in the world, and mean to die a proper Deist."

Strangely enough, the impetus for Beadle's insane belief that his family had to be spared ridicule from his failures in business by being horrifically slain was all a front for his evil—for, on the day William Beadle killed his family and took his own life, he was worth some "three hundred pounds sterling," a value that any other farmer in Connecticut at the time would not have exceeded.

CHAPTER 3

Seduced by the Devil

September 1821: Manchester, New Hampshire

ON THE MORNING OF APRIL 5, 1821, ESTHER COLLINS RAN TO the home of family friend and neighbor Daniel Davis Farmer. It was eight o'clock, Daniel later said, when he was summoned suddenly to Esther's sister Anna Ayer's house in nearby Goffstown, New Hampshire. Esther sounded alarmed. Whatever she needed, it was definitely urgent. Something was terribly wrong at Anna's house, and Daniel was told he needed to get over there right away.

"Mrs. Ayer, Daniel, she is . . . is"—Esther sounded out of breath and "much frightened"—". . . Anna and her daughter are much abused. I need you to go to Anna's house at once."

Daniel ran from his home to Anna's.

A day laborer by trade, Daniel had lived with his parents until he turned fourteen, when he up and moved in with a man, John Keyes, in Goffstown. He stayed six months with Keyes. Through that relationship, Daniel met and began working for Anna Ayer's husband, Joshua, who died years later from an unknown ailment. After Joshua was gone, Daniel bounced around Goffstown working as a hand.

Daniel was a rather mawkish, clean-cut man of "humble parentage, who were low in circumstances," said one writer. Daniel grew up in Derryfield, which would become known as Manchester, the largest city in New Hampshire and, by today's standards, the largest city in northern New England. Crime is rampant in Manchester these days. New Hampshire is, incidentally, one of those quintessential New England states made famous by its magnificent white-capped (rock ledge) mountains and breathtaking views of pine trees as tall and straight as big city buildings, green as broccoli, lined up by the thousands like arrows. There was a rock structure known as the Old Man of the Mountain (it has fallen into a pile of rubble recently), a ledge formation that, when viewed from the side, resembled, quite strikingly, the profile of an old man's face. Yet New Hampshire has developed a strong sense of community as it has grown from a produce-farming state into an agricultural center of dairy. Not a lot has changed in the state since the days when Daniel Farmer and Anna Ayer walked the streets. People are still cordial and kind. The pace of life is slow and steady, maybe even a bit lazy. Summer barbecues are held on town greens and still incorporate gazebos and potato sack races into the day's festivities. And fishing and hunting are the top two gaming sports residents and tourists enjoy most.

When Daniel Farmer was called upon by Esther, however, the most anyone had heard about crime was maybe a cow stolen for food, or a saloon brawl that had gotten out of hand. People worked hard in those days. They did not complain about poverty or the economy or the troubling aspects of life; they got up every morning and tried to make the best out of each and every day. You made do with what you had and prayed for a better tomorrow. Prayer, in fact, was an essential part of life—God still came first for a majority of Puritan-born and bred New Englanders.

Anna and Daniel had known each other because of the work Daniel had done for Anna's husband. Back in 1814, Daniel bought twenty acres of what was called "wild land" in Goffstown. He built a humble home and barn and, in 1814, married a local gal, Abigail

Hackett, who bore him four children. That past December (1820), Daniel had sold his property and moved to Derryfield. Apparently, he had gotten into a dispute with Anna over some landscaping he had done for her and decided to move away and be done with the woman. Their troubles, according to one writer, "were all passed over" when Daniel left town, but it should be noted that there was still a bit of hostility on Anna's part over a debt and Daniel's sudden departure.

There was also the hush-hush, rumored problem of an unborn, illegitimate child. That January, Anna made an accusation against Daniel, claiming he was the father of a child she was carrying. A happily married man, Daniel denied it.

As Daniel ran toward Anna's home, there could be no doubt (if you believe his version) that Daniel's mind was on Anna and her fourteen-year-old daughter's safety and well-being.

"I came to the house near [Anna's] and saw several people about it," Daniel recalled.

There was a crowd, indeed, hovering around the door. They were agitated and stirred up. This was the beginning of the end for Daniel Farmer.

Daniel came upon the doorway and saw that there were people talking and whispering and roaming around. It was there, when he "got within five or six feet of the door," Daniel remembered, "[that] I discovered blood, and a small stone lying on the ground (from four to six pounds weight), bloody, and hair clinging to it."

Stunned by this, Daniel ran for the door.

There was "blood on the sill—the casing of the door was bloody, one side of it much so."

Rushing into the house, Daniel was equally astonished—or was he?—to see even more blood on the wooden, dusty floor. The floor had burns on it too, Daniel later explained. Patches of black all over, as though there had been a fire put out just in time, before the remainder of the house could ignite and burn. "The floor was burnt in two places or more, and appeared as though burnt by coals of brands flung on."

The scene appeared horrific. Yet where were Anna and her daughter? With all this blood, it was clear to Daniel that someone had been hurt badly. Acclimating himself to the surroundings, Daniel looked over at the one bed in the room—and there lay the widow Anna Ayer.

"I saw a woman on [the bed] covered over," Daniel recalled.

Anna.

"Is she dead?" Daniel asked the neighbors and townspeople called to the scene. They were standing around Anna, hats clung to their chests, tears in their eyes, subdued and emotional.

"No," someone said.

Daniel approached. He moved the "clothes" covering Anna and knelt next to her bedside.

"She appeared in a sog [dazed], her eyes were closed," Daniel observed. Anna had been savagely beaten. Her face was swollen, her head and face smeared over with fresh and dried blood. There was yellow pus dripping down the side of her head covering.

"Do you know who I am?" Daniel asked.

"Yes," she said, "you are . . . Daniel. Daniel Farmer."

She was lying on her left side. Daniel removed part of the covering over Anna's head to have a look. There was what he later called a "deep wound" on the right side of Anna's forehead, "three to four inches long, one inch wide or more ..." From what Daniel could discern, it "looked deep [and] . . . appeared to be doubled in by the weapon."

Daniel went to remove the covering from the other side of her head, but someone stepped up and stopped him.

"No, you had better not, lest it should bleed," the man said sternly.

Daniel agreed. He stood, walked away from the bed, and looked around the room, trying to figure out what had happened. He spied a shovel on the floor, "bloody and much bent," he later reported. He walked over to the shovel and studied it, realizing how violent the attack on Anna must have been. The shovel, made of metal, had been broken. There was hair and blood stuck to it.

Anna had been beaten with a metal shovel, it appeared, but also, Daniel Farmer would soon learn, with a wooden club of some sort.

"I saw no club at that time," Daniel said later. "Next morning I found a club, broken into four pieces, part of it split. The club was two and a half feet long or more, one inch and a half in diameter, was maple, and appeared as though it had laid [sic] under water."

After studying the shovel, Daniel went back to Anna, who was rapidly fading.

"Who hurt you?" Daniel asked Anna. "Please tell me, Anna. You are near death, I'm sorry. Tell me, who hurt you?"

Anna did not motion or speak, according to Daniel's later testimony. "She did not say whether she understood me or not."

"You're dying, Anna. Please tell me," Daniel pleaded.

But Anna stopped talking at that point and could not gather her senses enough to explain what happened. There's a good chance Anna was slipping into a coma, her brain swelling, fluid around her brain dulling all her senses. With additional fluid leaking from her open skull wound, it was a wonder she could speak at all. She was clearly dying, and would soon be on her way toward heaven.

It was odd, some later said, that when Daniel Farmer told this story of seeing Anna Ayer on that day, he never mentioned Anna's daughter, who had also been beaten and, although her injuries were not life-threatening, was in another room recuperating from the same attack.

Some time later, after Daniel left, Esther's husband, Abner Collins, walked up to Anna as she lay dying and asked if she felt like she was going to make it much longer. Abner stood by Anna's bedside, certain that the woman in front of him was breathing her last.

"What is it, Anna? Do you express any hope of living?" Abner queried his neighbor.

Anna took a deep breath, Abner later said, and then spoke: "I shall hope to live long enough to see that devilish, damned Farmer hanged!"

Daniel?

Abner was shocked and dismayed by the revelation, but also certain what Anna had said.

Anna's mother was there during those days when Anna fought for her life and slowly slipped away. Abner found Mrs. Ayer and asked her if Anna had said anything in his absence. Had she talked about who attacked her before he arrived at the home?

"That devilish, damned Farmer," Anna's mother said.

"Did she say she had hoped to die—was she in that much pain?"

"She said she hoped, if God's will, she should not die by the hands of that man!"

Dr. William Wallace was the attending physician during those days when Anna slipped in and out of consciousness. He had seen people beaten before, but never like this. In those days before forensics and criminal profiling, what the doctor and those investigating this strange, apparently motiveless beating missed was that the person who had attacked Anna Ayer and her daughter was angrier than a grizzly watching someone messing with her cubs. The number of blows to Anna's head and the extent of the injuries indicated—though no one at the scene had really hit on this—that Anna's attacker knew her personally. Nothing in the house had been disturbed, as in a home invasion. Neither Anna nor her daughter had said anything about a man breaking in and wanting sex. They had been home, all indications appeared, and someone had walked in and beat them senselessly.

Wallace took one look at Anna and knew she did not have long. He later said she had a "one inch opening" in her skull. Anna's head had been smashed in and literally cracked open.

"I told her that her situation was dangerous and I thought it impossible for her to recover," Wallace later said.

Anna looked away and did not reply.

The doctor leaned down and examined Anna's wounds more closely, later noting that the extent of her injuries was fatal, but nobody around her seemed to realize.

"A piece of the skull on the right side," Wallace reported, "was broken off nearly as large as a cracker—the bone was raised from the *dura mater* [the milky white, balloonlike membrane covering the brain] nearly an inch. There must have been two blows on that section of the head. The *dura mater* appeared wounded or torn, but not perforated, more bruised or scratched. There was another wound over the left eye. I attended to her till death, and have no doubt her death was caused by the wound described."

Wallace was with Anna during her struggle to stay alive— which was to last, it turned out, a total of seven days. During that entire time, the doctor said, the Widow Ayer did not once mention that Daniel Davis Farmer was responsible for attacking her or her daughter.

◆

At the opening of the trial nearly six months after the Widow Anna Ayer died from her injuries, Attorney General George Sullivan began the proceedings by stating how, beyond anything else,

Daniel Davis Farmer, in murdering Anna Ayer and attacking her daughter, had been "seduced by the instigation of the Devil."

There it was: The devil made him do it—the conditional battle cry of the innocent man claiming insanity. It would seem, in studying this case and what Daniel Farmer himself later said, that if he did not kill the Widow Ayer, a ghost representing him might have—or maybe Daniel Farmer was in a complete black-out and, truly, did not recall what was an extremely violent episode against which he was now forced to defend himself. Either way, Farmer was facing a noose if convicted.

Daniel Farmer was not yet thirty years old as he stood, his grimy hands shackled tightly behind his back, facing a jury that held his life in their hands. The popular local man was being accused of bludgeoning the Widow Ayer in Goffstown, New Hampshire, with a "fifty-cent shovel" upon the side of her head, then beating her repeatedly with a wooden club, on top of attacking the Widow Ayer's daughter, fourteen-year-old Young Anna Ayer. By all means, this trial was the main attraction in the Goffstown region of New Hampshire. Thousands were said to have turned out to watch the proceedings, even more awaiting word of its outcome.

As the trial continued, Farmer gave his testimony of arriving at the Ayer property that night after being called upon by Abner Collins's wife, Esther. The day laborer described the layout of Anna's house and what he saw upon his arrival the following day: a bloody stone with hair on it, burn marks on the floor inside the house, Anna on her deathbed. All seemed to be going well for Farmer as he testified. He came across as believable and sincere. Other witnesses called after him backed up some of what he had said, while some pointed a finger directly at him.

The most effective testimony came from Young Anna Ayer herself, a witness to the crimes that had taken her mother from her.

The trial had been scheduled for the days just following Anna's death, but Young Anna had been injured so severely that the attorney general had had to postpone until his star witness could get her senses back and be strong enough to testify as to what she had seen and heard the night she and her mother were brutalized. That terrible night had been embedded in Young Anna Ayer's mind. The child said she could never forget it.

The tragedy had begun on the brisk spring afternoon of April 4, 1821. Daniel Farmer had been stewing about Anna all afternoon, according to a witness. He had in fact become quite obsessed with the woman and had been drinking heavily that day. One person said Daniel had gone to William Riddle's local general store in the village of Piscataquog and purchased "a pint of rum and a few crackers." Several in town had claimed to have seen Daniel leave Riddle's and head toward Anna's property.

Young Anna Ayer picked up the narrative from there, describing to jurors how she answered a knock at the door about nine o'clock at night. Young Anna had been sewing. Her mother had been fiddling around the house finishing her daily chores.

"I want to come in," Daniel said. Young Anna recognized the voice behind the door immediately.

Young Anna did not want this heathen inside her home, she said, but her mother walked over to the door and, telling Young Anna to step aside, allowed Daniel to enter, explaining to her daughter, "Go back to your sewing now, child."

Daniel walked in and was clearly drunk. He stumbled and stuttered. He had that bottle of rum, now almost empty, in one hand, the other hand apparently keeping him steady as he found his way into the home. Unshaven, with terrible odors coming from his person, Daniel mumbled a few words neither

Anna nor her daughter could understand, and walked into the living chamber.

"Have a drink with me, Anna!" Daniel suggested, demanding the elder Ayer woman have a toast with him. It was clear from his tone that Daniel was not going to be taking no for an answer.

Anna thought about it.

"If I must, Daniel."

Young Anna said her mother took "drink some three times" while Young Anna, sitting in a rocker, sewing quietly, looked on.

They stayed in the chamber for a short time, chit-chatting. Then Daniel said, "Go outdoors with me, Anna." He was acting strangely, according to Young Anna. Daniel wanted something, no doubt about it. They'd had a past and it was said by many—chiefly Anna Ayer—that she was carrying Daniel's child.

Anna walked outdoors with Daniel.

"They were gone nine to ten minutes," Young Anna later remembered.

When they came back into the home (Anna following behind Daniel), Daniel had a maple club in his hand, which he must have left outside by the door before walking in earlier. Young Anna watched, wondering what he was doing with the club. The presence of the thing scared her.

"It was as large as a chair post," Young Anna reported.

Daniel then set the club down on the mantel of the fireplace. There was never any discussion regarding the reason behind why Daniel brought the club inside the home with him, or if Anna or her daughter felt intimidated by the presence of such an odd object. Young Anna said her mother and Daniel were not arguing at this time. There was, as she put, "no anger between them" at that moment.

They sat in the chamber, the club there in the room beside Daniel like a cane. The booze, one might assume, was beginning to have a deleterious effect on Daniel as he stared at Anna, she giving it right back to him. If there was one thing that was common within all the testimony given about Anna, it would be that she was not a woman who would have taken any guff from a drunken bully like Daniel Farmer. Anna had a reputation, good or bad, for standing on her own two feet and not backing down from anyone.

But there was growing animosity between the two. Anna was hoping to have a drink with Daniel and maybe satisfy his needs—whatever they were—and then send him on his way. Could it have been that Anna was threatening to go to Daniel's wife with news that she was carrying Daniel's baby? There was never any mention about this subject by Young Anna.

Daniel had other plans, however, according to Young Anna's testimony.

"I'm going to kill you!" Daniel stood and shouted for no apparent reason. Then he walked over to where he had placed his club and, putting on a "pair of mittens," grabbed hold of the maple club and lifted it above his head.

Anna tried to stand, saying she was, in turn, going to kill Daniel.

Like a logger pulling back with an axe, Daniel heaved the club behind him, swung as hard as he could, and subsequently struck Anna square about the head, knocking her violently and bloodily to the floor.

"You are killing my mother!" Young Anna jumped up and screamed—this, mind you, as Anna fell to the ground, her head opening up, blood spurting all over the wooden floor. Daniel had struck the woman hard enough to knock her out cold.

Young Anna, realizing Daniel had effectively snapped (he was no longer himself; she could sense it and see it in his eyes) and was not going to stop, ran for the door so as to hopefully escape and seek help for her dying mother.

But Daniel chased the young lass and, without warning, using his club once again, knocked Young Anna down on the ground with a quick blow to the back of the head.

And that was about all Young Anna remembered.

Running.

Screaming.

Feeling the weight of that maple club impact her skull.

Then darkness.

Young Anna came to some time later (she had no idea how long she had been unconscious). "The first thing I remember after receiving the blow, I was lying on the floor near the bed, not in the place where I was knocked down," she recalled, "[and] I did not recollect that he struck me or my mother more than once."

Young Anna was having trouble, now dazed and rattled by such a powerful blow, understanding what was going on in front of her. The violence had happened so quickly.

From the evidence left behind at the crime scene, it's clear that Anna's attacker struck the woman more than once, but maybe left Young Anna alone after that first blow.

As she got her senses back from being smashed about the head, Young Anna watched out of the corner of her eye as Daniel took pieces of clothing, lit them on fire, and scattered the burning remnants all about the floor. Then, he took several coal embers from the crackling fireplace and spread them throughout the room. Daniel Farmer, according to the one witness in the room that night with him and Anna, tried to burn up both Young Anna and her mother, who was completely unconscious at this point and bleeding profusely from her head wounds.

Young Anna thought the only way to survive was to feign a more serious injury and hope this madman left the house without finishing her off. She watched as the embers caught various pieces of furniture and the wood flooring.

"It was moving closer to the bed," where her mother was struggling to breathe, lying on the floor, not moving. "Two chairs were on fire."

The young girl kept still, hoping, praying that Farmer did not find out she was not as injured as she appeared. "Soon, Farmer left the house."

Young Anna jumped up and secured the door latch with the back of an axe and a nail, then immediately doused the flames with blankets.

It didn't work.

She then spied a bucket in the center of the room and ran to it.

It had no water inside—Daniel had emptied it before leaving.

She didn't have time to run outside to the well.

Frantically, Young Anna searched the house and came up with "some beer that was in a pot in the corner."

After extinguishing the fire, Anna helped her mother up onto the bed. Then she covered her with blankets before plopping down next to her, exhausted from her exertions and still dizzy from that blow she had taken to the head.

<hr />

This testimony by young Anna Ayer was devastating to Daniel Farmer. He had said he was not even in Anna's house that night. Yet, here was an eyewitness—a young girl who had been beaten herself and took a half-year to recover from those injuries.

Another witness came forward and tightened the noose even more, giving jurors a motive. Thomas Hardy, a local man who knew Daniel and had spent some time with him before the murder, spoke harsh words against his former friend.

"Have you ever heard the prisoner express any ill will towards the deceased?" the solicitor asked Hardy on October 9, 1821, as he sat in the witness box inside the local Goffstown meetinghouse during the trial.

Thomas Hardy spoke assuredly, recalling, "Sometime in February or March I heard him say, if he could ever 'find her two rods from anybody, he would kill her.'"

"Was the prisoner sober?"

"Yes!"

Later, Hardy added one more blow to Daniel Farmer's case, enlightening the trial room with this gem: "I stated that Farmer said that he would be damned if he did not kill the Widow Ayer, if he found her two rods from any person—and that I cautioned him against making such a declaration. He said she had abused him by laying a child to him wrongfully."

Motive. Hardy's testimony indicated that Daniel had been so all-consumed with the idea that Anna had started this vicious rumor about him fathering a child with her, if he ever stood in the same room with the woman, he would surely kill her for sullying his reputation and trying to destroy his marriage, a household he had built with a wife he was said to have loved deeply, along with the four children she had given him.

Hardy was asked his opinion about Anna, and if he had, in fact, instigated Daniel and maybe gotten him excited, putting pressure on him to get Anna back for her misdeeds and gossiping.

"Did you not tell Farmer," the solicitor queried, "when conversing with him about the Widow Ayer, that if you were in his place, *you* would kill her?"

Thomas Hardy did not hold back: "I told him if any such dirty creature as she was should swear a young one on me, I would cut her damned head off!"

"Are you not in the habit of swearing at your children, and threatening to kill them?" the solicitor asked as a final question.

"I sometimes get into a passion," Hardy responded with a smile, "but mean no harm."

Daniel Farmer's lawyer tried to argue the notion that there had not been anyone the prosecution called as a witness who could prove the Widow Ayer had died from the wounds she had received to her head. So the question the lawyer posed became: Had anyone even scratched the surface of the proposition that the Widow Ayer could have been deathly ill before this purported "blow to the head"?

It was almost as if Farmer's legal counsel was trying to make the claim that someone else might have given Anna the final blows (or she had done them to herself), because there had been no doctor who could state emphatically that the blows Anna Ayer sustained on that night were fatal.

Daniel Farmer's defense called several character witnesses to try to support Daniel's argument that he was a good country boy who could not possibly have lost his temper and murdered this woman. He was called "a man of mild and friendly feelings" who "never engaged in any quarrels." He was said to have been an "industrious and regular" man with a "mild and calm" demeanor. One witness called Daniel "remarkably domestic," a fellow who was "attentive to his own business." He was said to have taken care of his mother as she got on in years, giving the old woman several wonderful years, putting food in her belly, clothes on her back, a roof over her head. "His general character and conduct is good," said Elisha Quinby, a friend. "I never saw him out of humor. . . . I never saw anything malicious in him, and never heard it suggested that he was so."

In they came, one after the other, claiming to have known Daniel for seven years, eight and nine, ten, twelve years, since he was a child, even fifteen and sixteen years.

"He is a good neighbor, and I never thought his temper bad," said Abner Collins, in a total 180-degree turn from what he had said about Daniel earlier that day as a prosecution witness.

William Riddle testified that Daniel never bought any rum that afternoon. Riddle, who ran his general store and knew every customer on a first-name basis, called Daniel a man of "good character" who came to visit his store on that fateful day and left "about sunset."

Several witnesses testified that Daniel had never, as far as they knew, said anything good, bad, or indifferent about the Widow Ayer.

He never mentioned the woman!

Then the attack on Anna began—that is, Young Anna, the prosecution's star witness. Isaac Flanders, a neighbor, said Anna was "not good. General report is, she is not to be believed—her character was always considered bad."

Sally Palmer sat down for one question. Daniel's attorney wanted to know if Young Anna's mother, the Widow Ayer, had been ill *before* April 4, 1821.

Palmer said, "She [Anna] complained the summer before."

Young Anna was re-called.* There had been some indication that Young Anna had decorated the court proceedings with several fabrications, and Daniel Farmer's lawyer wanted to clear a few things up.

"Do you know, Anna, how the blood happened to be on the axe handle?"

"Yes!" the child said without hesitation. "I bloodied it when I took hold of it to drive the nail over the latch of the door."

After a few additional inconsequential questions, Young Anna was allowed to step down.

Then Dr. Wallace was recalled to the shock of the room.

"Did you examine the Widow Anna Ayer after her decease?"

"I did," the doctor testified.

---

* During this day and age trials were a bit more fluid than they are today. Witnesses were called and recalled, called back a third or even fourth or fifth time to answer one or two questions the attorneys thought pertinent in light of any new information brought out by previous witnesses.

"Was she pregnant?"

"She was not. And there was no appearance of her having been so."

"Was it generally believed in the neighborhood that the Widow Ayer was *not* pregnant?"

"Yes."

In his closing, Daniel Farmer's attorney argued that Anna had "carried with her, to the last moments of her life, a deadly hatred and spite against" Daniel that had, over a period of time, turned into a revenge-filled game of her being ill and near death, and she and her daughter getting together to concoct a story about Daniel coming to the house to kill her. This diabolical plot was described as some sort of final ploy to get Daniel back for not responding to Anna's romantic advances. Some claimed Anna hated Daniel because he did not want to be with her. Because of this, when she became ill and realized she was dying, she desired to repay him by framing him for her murder! Perhaps Anna, Daniel's lawyer suggested, wanted to spend eternity with Daniel and figured this was the only way.

"Gentlemen, it is painful and afflicting to me to say anything against this unfortunate girl. Her situation truly demands commiseration. . . . Her present character is wholly the fault of her education. This is her misfortune which deserves compassions rather than censure."

Daniel's lawyer wasn't talking about the Widow Anna Ayer; he was referring to the prosecution's most damaging witness, Young Anna. The only way to win this case was to defame the reputation of this one witness. Young Anna was either going to be believed or not.

The prosecution was given its turn to argue a case for guilt. The tall and slender solicitor began with a plea of how difficult this case must be for the community to hear. "On your verdict is suspended the fate of a fellow citizen," the prosecutor stated. He spared no drama when grounding the trial in the reality of the moment, adding, "Whether he shall be permitted to live, or whether he shall be cut off from society and consigned to the mansions of the dead, it belongs to you to determine."

From that point on the prosecutor stuck to the facts: One, that a witness had come in and told a tale of murder from her firsthand account; and two, that no one could destroy Young Anna's reputation, calling her a lying lass who made up stories. You believe Young Anna and Daniel should be marched to the gallows, the prosecutor seemed to say. You don't believe Anna, he articulated rather well, and you still have additional witnesses who testified that Anna, on her deathbed, had fingered Daniel for the crime.

Either way, the slick prosecutor said, you must find this man guilty!

By the time both sides were finished on October 9, 1821, it was eleven o'clock in the evening. The trial had gone all day and all night.

The judge asked the jury to retreat into seclusion for deliberation and come back with a verdict.

If this had been a railroad job by the prosecution (as some have suggested), well, that steam engine was barreling down the tracks at hyper speed—because it took the jury all of one hour to come back with its expected verdict. By midnight, the eighteen men chosen to hear this case had walked back into the meetinghouse and announced that they had unanimously found Daniel Farmer guilty of first-degree murder.

The attorney general wasted no time and soon moved to have Daniel Davis Farmer, shocked and stunned by this travesty of justice, executed for his crimes.

The Honorable Justice Levi Woodbury spoke next, announcing that he would hand down his sentence the following morning. Everyone was to go home, get some much-needed rest, and then return at the nine o'clock hour on the next day to hear of Daniel Farmer's fate.

It was a bright and noticeably warm Friday morning, taking into consideration that it was October in New England. Judge Levi Woodbury was back running his court inside the meetinghouse. The building was filled to capacity. Men were dressed in their Sunday best whilst the women wore wide-brimmed hats and puffy dresses, and whispered and chatted with gossipy gestures as the lawyers from both sides walked in.

Daniel Farmer, one could argue, did not look so good after having not slept a wink the previous night, no doubt contemplating how his life had come down to this one day when it seemed the world was closing in around him. What had he done to deserve such a mortal wound to his soul?

It was clear after the judge spoke that he had thought long and hard about this speech (if one night to consider it was enough time) and that he understood it was his turn now to enjoy fifteen minutes and take part in solidifying his place in this drama forever.

"It is with emotions of deep compassion," Judge Levi stated as the crowd hushed and settled in to listen, "I am about to pronounce against you the judgment of the law." Levi stared arrogantly at Daniel Farmer, his gaze magnified by the quiet taking over the room.

Levi went on to use big words and drawn-out phrases simpler language could have wrapped up in a mere few sentences. He talked of the horrors of Daniel's offense, the unbridled tarnish Daniel had placed on the reputations of "the lisping tenderness of your children" and wife, and how Daniel had, more than anything, "offended God in the skies." The crime was a "peculiar turpitude and atrocity," Levi added at one point, sounding bored with his own choice of words.

Daniel Farmer, so said the judge, had "imbrued his hands in human blood in a manner of the most premeditated." And then, when the crowd thought he could not be any more dramatic than he had been already, Judge Levi unloaded, saving the best for last:

> These reflections on your deplorable destiny excite such commiseration in us as almost to disarm my tongue from its duty. But the great interests of Society, whose peace you have disturbed, whose laws you have invaded and profaned, and whose future tranquility you endanger are not to be betrayed. . . . Listen, therefore, and reflect with solemnity as the sword of human justice trembles over you; the dread sentence must be speedily executed, and then you launch into an unknown world; the fate of your immortal soul is sealed forever. Let me therefore exhort . . . [that] you stand at the eternal bar of Christ that you seize upon the salvation by his cross. I can say no more except to pronounce the judgment of the law, which is: that you be taken hence to prison, from prison to the place of execution, and there hung by the neck until you are dead, and may the God of Compassion have mercy upon your soul.

Daniel Davis Farmer was taken to that dark and desolate place on December 3, 1821, to be executed. The execution was to occur in Amherst, New Hampshire, a fifteen-mile hike south of Goffstown. The delay between the sentencing and the execution had been caused by the town's need to build the gallows especially for Daniel Farmer's execution. What's more, the governor of New Hampshire, talking about how disturbing and outlandish the circumstances surrounding the case were, not to mention the frenzied interest in the affair, granted a one-month reprieve to the defendant in order to go through the testimony and evidence himself to make sure the right man was being hanged.

As he waited for that day, Daniel Farmer wrote letters to relatives, his wife, mother and sister, and a friend, John Gould, who lived in Dunbarton, ten miles north of Goffstown. According to the content of these letters and one writer's study of them (copies of which are hard to come by, if they even exist any longer), Daniel underwent "a wonderful change of heart and perfectly resigned to meet death." He had accepted his fate, apparently, and was resigned to die at the hand of the state for a crime in which he claimed he had no part.

The Reverend Nathan Lord was brought in as Daniel's spiritual advisor. Lord was pastor of the Congregational Church in Amherst, and would become, in the decades ahead, the president of Dartmouth College.

As December 3, 1821, came to pass, the town still wasn't ready for Daniel Farmer's execution, so it wasn't until Thursday, January 3, 1822, at 2:30 in the afternoon, that Daniel Farmer was brought to the gallows erected just south of the Amherst town common for the sole purpose of this day.

Ten thousand people were on hand to witness Daniel Farmer's death by hanging. The day was arctic cold. One report claimed that "every available space, including the roofs of nearby buildings, was occupied." One such building, with so many people standing atop and shuffling to get the best view, could not sustain the weight and collapsed amid screams.

With the crowd settled, the execution commenced. Four deputy sheriffs rode into town on horseback. Make no mistake about it: This was a spectacle as much as a sentence. New Hampshire was making a statement here. You don't kill a defenseless woman and live to talk about it.

Then Benjamin Pierce, the "high sheriff of the county," arrived, before Daniel Farmer, along with Reverend Lord and a colleague of the clergyman, two deputies, one on each side of Daniel, was whisked in on "a double sleigh."

Underneath the carriage transporting Daniel and his spiritual advisers, for the entire crowd to see, was the coffin in which Daniel would be buried directly after death settled on him.

Surrounding the carriage was a display of law enforcement hubris. There were a reported four deputies on horseback on the right side following along, four deputies on horseback on the left, and four deputies on horseback tagging along at the rear. Watching this display of pomp and circumstance, you'd think Daniel Farmer had assassinated the president of the United States.

Daniel Farmer walked slowly up the stairs toward the rope with his name on it. The actual death warrant was read for the crowd. Then the Reverend Lord offered a prayer, "in which the prisoner joined," said a prison report of the day.

The executioner then placed "the fatal rope" around Daniel's neck.

"At that time he seemed to be suffering severely from the effects of the cold," said that prison report, "[and so the] Rev. Mr. Lord stepped forward, and taking his cloak from his shoulders, placed it over him. A handkerchief was given him with the directions to drop it when he was ready. He uttered a silent prayer, closed in a firm and audible voice, gave the signal, and the drop fell."

The doors opened and Daniel Farmer fell through, his neck snapping loudly in the silence of the crowd.

"He hung about twenty minutes," the report continued, "and by the surgeons present was pronounced dead. His remains were taken down and delivered to his brother, who conveyed them to Manchester, where they were buried on the following Sunday. A large audience attended his funeral, and a sermon was delivered."

As the years passed, controversy and rumor surrounded this incredible New England murder story. In fact, the *Boston Gazette,* a popular nineteenth-century newspaper (or tabloid, perhaps), reported, "We understand Farmer, who to have been executed . . . for the murder of Anna Ayer, died in Amherst jail."

Like many scandalous stories of the day, especially those with murder at the center, erroneous reports circulated to add to the stigma, drama, and folklore. If we cannot trust the word of—collectively— ten thousand people on hand to witness an execution, whose version can we believe?

But then we have to ask: Was Young Anna Ayer lying, or did Daniel Farmer murder her mother?

We will never know for certain.

CHAPTER 4

Better Off in Heaven

June 1879: Holyoke, Massachusetts

HOLYOKE WAS KNOWN FOR MUCH OF THE NINETEENTH CENTURY as a growing textile and paper mill city built by immigrant and migrant labor forces that had flocked to Western Massachusetts during the early 1800s in hopes of beginning a new life in America. Along a narrow pathway at the city's edge is a fifty-seven-foot drop down into the Connecticut River at a place called South Hadley Falls, the initial incentive to build an industrial city based around that massive display of Mother Nature, an energy force of running water that could power a major portion of the city's machines.

"As Holyoke matured," city historians later noted, "it began to diversify industrially. Four and a half miles of canals were dug by pick and shovel through the lower wards, and all types of products were manufactured along their banks. Steam pumps, blank books, silk goods, hydrants, bicycles, and trolleys were among a growing list of goods being shipped all over the world."

This was a city full of promise, full of ingenuity and vigor, full of contentment for what an industrialized world could provide a populace growing in numbers no one could quite keep up with.

Right around the 1870s, however, as a second wave of migration came from Canada in the north and the Irish from the south and Boston, this once-booming industrial city hit a downturn in economic development. There just wasn't enough money in the city for builders to develop new infrastructure. Scores of men and even women were now looking for work. For some, finding a job in other parts of New England and moving from Holyoke fed the family and kept life moving forward—these were common, everyday people who went with the ebb and flow of life and found a way to bounce back from any misfortune. For John Kemmler, who lost his job at Germania Mills, a textile factory in South Holyoke that specialized in wool, having to support three children became a burden Kemmler never thought he'd have to endure.

Kemmler had just returned to Holyoke in June 1879 after spending nearly six months in Denver, having "deserted his family," he said when he returned, to go and look for work out west, taking with him their entire family savings of $260. It's more likely that John Kemmler was too drunk to recall exactly the reason why he left his wife and kids with nothing; nonetheless, he was back in New England now and looking for a job in town.

A German, born in Wittenberg in 1831, Kemmler returned to Holyoke in 1879, and by that time he had been in the states for seventeen years. It's safe to speculate that Kemmler, by then, knew how America operated and the opportunities available for a man who wanted to work hard and support his family. Kemmler had studied medicine; but had "always," claimed an 1879 *New York Times* article about him, "been in poor circumstances."

The Kemmlers lived in an attic room in what was called the Germania Corporation block, or what the *Times* referred to as "comparative poverty." Many factories had made housing for their workers available in a location close to the main production facility, but lots of these places—not only in Holyoke, but all over New England—were squalid and run down, low rent domains corporations forced upon workers because of the low wages they paid out. On this particular day in June 1879, Kemmler was told by corporate that not only would he never work for Germania again, but that it was high time he moved his three children and wife out of his attic apartment.

The children ranged in age from six years to fifteen months. Two of the three girls were twins, Annie and Amy. The toddler went by the name Ludmiller.

Kemmler and his wife, while the children played, stood in the kitchen and talked that afternoon. It was close to two o'clock. Kemmler had just been given the news that he had to leave the apartment by the end of the day and did not know how to explain this to his wife.

"Go up the street," Kemmler finally ordered her, "and buy a hat" for the youngest child.

A strange request.

The children were up in a living room area of the attic apartment. Kemmler said he'd look after them while she was gone.

"Go now . . . move along. Do what I tell you."

Mrs. Kemmler grabbed her purse, fixed her hair, and walked out the door.

Certain his wife was gone, Kemmler went into the room where his three young children were gathered.

"I have some candy for you all upstairs," he said lovingly, like a dad. "Will you come with me?"

Before they went up the stairs, Kemmler had prepared a meal for the children: gruel. On this day, however, he had added one special flavoring.

Cyanide of potassium.

John Kemmler, a forty-eight-year-old unemployed father of three, was going to murder his children because he was too ashamed to go on living a life of struggle and having nowhere left to live. He thought it was the only way out of the situation in which so many had found themselves during a tough economic period in New

England, when jobs were becoming as scarce as a good meal. What Kemmler never realized—and maybe he was too damn proud or psychotic to see it—was that an Industrial Revolution was just over the horizon, and New England business would once again thrive and prosper.

When they got upstairs Kemmler "made one of the girls" take a teaspoon full of the gruel. He had laced the nasty mush with so much poison, however, that it made the child vomit.

Realizing it would be impossible for him to kill his three children in this manner, Kemmler came up with a second idea.

"You," he said stoically, "come here."

He took one of the twins by the arm and violently dragged her into the "front bedroom." Kemmler never said whether he spoke to any of the children at this point, but he took out his pistol and, without warning, shot the child in the back of the head behind the earlobe.

She died instantly.

"The other twin he took into the rear bedroom and shot in a like manner, leaving her body on the floor," the *Times* reported the following day.

With her two sisters now dead, a fifteen-month-old, confused and likely crying, unknowingly awaited her turn to enter heaven.

Kemmler took the youngest, picked her up, placed her face down on the bed in the same room, put a pillow over the back of her tiny skull, and fired two muffled shots, one behind each ear, "burning the pillow in each case."

Staring at the bodies one last time, Kemmler locked the door to his apartment behind him and walked to Blaise Borten's Saloon just down the block.

There is no confirmed report of Kemmler ordering any liquor; instead, he walked into the saloon and paced back and forth in front of Borten's regular patrons already inside, men who were bellied up to the bar, looking at this strange man in a fit of agitation before them.

"Apparently in great trepidation, for 20 minutes," according to the *Times*, Kemmler walked back and forth inside the bar and talked to himself in whispers.

When he finished, Kemmler had a beer and, without emotion, said, "Borten, come with me outside."

The saloon owner and Kemmler retreated to the pavement near the establishment's entrance.

John Kemmler finally spoke. Handing Borten his tenement key, the broken man said, "I have just killed my three children. I have taken my last glass of beer."

Having said those remarkable words, Kemmler turned and "walked uptown."

Mrs. Kemmler soon returned, perhaps at the same time Borten went to the apartment to see what Kemmler was talking about, and if what he had spoken held any truth.

"Mrs. Kemmler was completely overcome by the loss of her children, and was taken in charge by friends," the *Times* reported.

Inside the apartment, two of the children lay dead, one in each of the bedchambers. Yet the third child, the youngest, was still alive when Borten reached her. John Kemmler thought he had finished the child off, but apparently he had not.

Was it possible she could survive?

At three o'clock that same day, John Kemmler was drinking in Martin Smith's Saloon uptown. He made no indication that he was trying to hide from what he had done; only that he was in need of some suds to drown out the demons inside his head. By this time, word had spread that Kemmler had attacked his three children in one swift afternoon of cold-blooded murder because he was too damned ashamed to face life ahead without being able to provide for them.

A man in the saloon, Adolph Engle, who had heard what Kemmler did, grabbed a hold of Kemmler and walked the murderer down to Deputy Sheriff Kingsbury's office just around the corner from the saloon.

Engle explained to the sheriff what was going on.

Sheriff Kingsbury searched Kemmler. He found the weapon, with four chambers emptied of their ammunition, and a piece of paper inscribed with three chilling words: CYANIDE OF POTASSIUM.

Kingsbury wasn't taking any chances, especially with evidence now backing up what had been said about town. He locked Kemmler up in a cell until he could further investigate the matter.

Just then, not showing any type of remorse or condemnation for his actions, Kemmler, in a state of insanity, perhaps, admitted what he had done. He was, the *Times* reported, "perfectly tractable, expressing willingness to let the law take its course."

The sheriff and Mr. Engle were shocked by the man's admissions. Even more, Kemmler gave a reason why he had committed such a heinous crime, knowing full well that the town would surely want his neck at the end of a noose. He began by "arguing with most cold-blooded philosophy," saying, "I have been out of work and could not then make both ends meet, even if I had something to do! My fear was that if the girls grew up, they might be led astray. They would be happier," Kemmler belted loudly from behind bars, "in heaven."

The men stood in disbelief at this man justifying the homicides of three children with such shallow words.

"I have been meditating on this crime for ten days," Kemmler admitted. "I, too, want to die now. I intended . . . I truly did, to kill myself after them, but seeing their dead forms, I shrank from it."

There was no need, it appeared, to investigate further. Kemmler admitted his crimes and knew what his sentence would be.

As the night passed, someone walked into the jail and explained to Kemmler as he sat on his cot that his youngest, Ludmiller, had survived so far and was now fighting for her life.

Kemmler, shocked by this revelation, stood and ran toward the bars of his cell in a rage. Shaking the bars, Kemmler lashed out, saying, "Might I get out of here and finish the job!"

He screamed this horrifying phrase over and again.

"Listen, listen to me," the man said as Kemmler seemed to calm down and sit down, "the child will not live . . . trust me."

Kemmler was a dirty man, unkempt, his clothing wrinkled and filthy. He was "medium in size, [and] has a broad, impassive face," reported the newspapers. "His eyes are far apart." Furthermore, he "wears a mustache and chin whiskers." As reporters sought to speak to Kemmler, they noticed one important factor about his demeanor: John Kemmler, sleeping soundly through the night after murdering his children, ate a hearty meal the following morning and showed "no remorse for his crime . . . [while] express[ing] a readiness to meet his fate."

"He says he is Protestant, but has not attended church since he lived in Holyoke," the *Times* reported.

The medical examiner conducted his inquest and, "having no trouble arriving at a verdict," deemed the girls' deaths by gunshot wounds, the manner homicide. Ludmiller hung on until 9:00 a.m. that following morning and then succumbed to her traumatic head wounds. The children were buried by the city a day later.

Before he was hanged for his heinous crimes, John Kemmler, oddly, wrote a letter to the wife of an overseer inside the German Mills where he had once worked. As the letter surfaced after his crimes, it was clear that he had written the letter before he murdered his children. Kemmler never wrote to his wife. Nevertheless,

Kemmler set out in this one letter to give further explanation of his behavior:

What I have done is the last act of my life. I wish I could have died to-day. I give up life because of its trouble. I went West . . . to begin another life, but could not, because I couldn't forget my children. I went into business with a partner, but couldn't stay, and returned to Holyoke to wind up my family affairs, poison my children, and shoot myself through the chest. This life is not worth living for any longer, and I can't live without my children. My wife knows nothing about this—she believes we are going away.

As New England murders go, this case was particularly chilling to Northeasterners because of its audacity, inhumanity, and crushed innocence. The locals referred to the Kemmler murders at the time as the "most exciting local tragedy" in Holyoke history, the "coolest and most deliberately brutal murders on record." And, as timeless as it sounds (for this crime is still in the news today as the economy struggles to rebound), it was purportedly spurred by a warped man who lost his job. How many times have we heard this story?

CHAPTER 5

Forged in Blood:
The New England Mafia Comes of Age

December 1931: Boston, Massachusetts

THE WOMAN SAT BEHIND HER DESK DOING WHAT RECEPTIONISTS do, totally ignorant of the fact that, within the next few moments, the framework of the Mafia in Boston—and all of New England, for that matter—would undergo a remarkable quick-change right in front of her.

For much of the early part of the twentieth century in Boston, organized crime had been managed and manhandled strictly and violently under the auspices of the local Southie Irish cliques of mobsters and wiseguys, the most revered and reviled known as the Gustin Gang. These were men who did not bother with cheap talk or idle threats; you messed with this organized bunch of Irish thugs in Boston and you wound up with cement shoes swimming with the smallmouth bass and eels in the Charles "Dirty Water" River.

On December 2, 1931, near downtown, the dynamic of the entire organized crime scene was to be transformed by bloodshed—the means of communication for the mob that seemed to speak loudest. Leader of the Irish mob, Frankie Wallace, along with two of his cohorts, had been invited to a meeting at the office of fellow Boston gangster Joseph Lombardo, the Italian rival to Wallace's Irish gang. The impetus for the meeting, according to Lombardo, was his concern that the Gustin Gang had gone on too much of a hijacking spree lately (mainly liquor from incoming ships in Boston Harbor). One cannot, Joey had made it clear, keep pilfering the pot—or the pot runs dry. Then again, if one *insists* on routinely taking from that pot, he had better divvy up those proceeds accordingly with your fellow Mafioso in town or . . .

Well, or else!

Lombardo wanted his piece of the hijacked pie; yet, it should be noted here that this was not what he had truly called Frankie to the meeting to "discuss." Joey Lombardo had other plans on this cold and dark afternoon in Boston's North End.

Frankie brought two of his just-in-case guys as shadows, Barney "Dodo" Walsh and Tim Coffey. Barney was a protector and nasty fellow, a man who shot first and never bothered to ask questions after. Coffey, not all that different, went along with whatever his boss told him. Unbeknownst to Lombardo, Frankie had decided he was not about to cut Lombardo and his gang in on anything extra. Thus, Frankie was actually heading over to the meeting to "dictate terms" of his Irish stronghold in the city, according to *The Underboss*, by Gerard O'Neill and Dick Lehr. If Lombardo thought he wanted a share of the enormous loads of booze the Gustin Gang had been hijacking by land and sea, then the Gustin boys would explain to him that he had another thing coming.

From Lombardo's perspective—and, notably, that of the eight men he had waiting with him behind the closed doors of his importing company—the time to make good with old scores had come and gone. Lombardo now wanted his piece of the pie in an entirely different currency. The mob in Boston was about to go through one of a few ethnic vicissitudes it would endure throughout the centuries —once again with that type of shoot-'em-up brutal violence the boys in Chicago and New York (Lucky Luciano, Al Capone, Meyer Lansky, Dutch Schultz, Mad Dog Coll, and Frank Nitti) had made famous already. Boston's crime syndicates were always considered the "poor stepsisters" to the likes of those highly organized and efficient gangs in the two bigger cities; but on this day, Joey Lombardo and his crew would hold a candle to their brethren—and send a direct message to anyone looking to nudge in on what Lombardo and his men believed was rightfully theirs.

~ ~

As that mild-mannered receptionist sat behind her desk inside Boston's Testa Building, she heard some sort of a commotion going on outside the door.

She got up from behind her desk. "Now, what is going on out there?"

This sort of professional building wasn't accustomed to rambunctious behavior in the hallways by men acting as children. It was quiet here. Serene, even. A place of white-collar business meetings and companies that knew their place among the likes of gangland stock such as Lombardo and his "importing" business.

The two gangs had met on the third floor inside the Testa Building. As Wallace and Dodo entered the room, Coffey not far behind, Lombardo and his fellow Mafioso waited. Then, what would become known as the Testa Building Massacre was over in a flash. Without warning, Lombardo and his crew unloaded sheets of gunfire like slanted rain as Wallace and his cronies entered, half-expecting this sort of barrage, one might reckon.

Dodo ran down a stairway nearby and was quickly pursued by several of Lombardo's men, who subsequently mowed him down in ribbons of ammunition as he tried to make it to the second floor. Within moments, Dodo lay face-down and dead on the landing of the stairs between the two floors.

Frankie Wallace rushed down those same stairs and made it to the second floor, where he burst into the aforementioned office space, startling the hell out of the receptionist while grabbing himself, falling, and dying, bloodying a reception chair.

Coffey was the only smart one: He had escaped the hail of gunfire, found a closet, and hid out until the cops came.

These men—top Gustin Gang soldiers—had been wiped out of the picture within seconds. And with that, the Italians had taken control of organized crime in Boston. This was the death of a generation of Irish Mafioso, inspiring, according to some, the award-winning Hollywood film starring Jack Nicholson, *The Departed*. It would be nearly thirty years from that point—with institutional organized crime names like Bulger and Flemmi at the helm—before the Irish would be back on top of Boston's crime scene. As Gerard O'Neill and Dick Lehr so appropriately put it in their book, *Black Mass: The Irish Mob, the FBI, and a Devil's Deal*, this was an "audacious" move on Joey Lombardo's part, perhaps sending organized crime in Boston into a new realm and setting in stone the gang's future: "Prior to the Gustin Gang ambush," Lehr and O'Neill wrote, "the Boston Mafia had been viewed as the puny pushcart peddlers of organized crime, a bush-league embarrassment compared to Al Capone's Chicago and Lucky Luciano's New York."

No more would Boston's mobsters be the laughingstock of the underworld. After Lombardo's little ambush, he turned and handed off the torch, and now there was a new name up in mob lights throughout Boston: BUCCOLA. Phil "Filippo" Buccola, a fight promoter from Italy who had taken over and decided to run things the "old school" way—which would, of course, end up causing Buccola problems of his own down the road.

❦

Beantown, as it has become known, had grown into a city that lived under an Irish credo until that day in December 1931 when Joey Lombardo and his crew gunned down Frankie Wallace and his henchmen. The Prohibition Era—from 1920 to 1933, a time when, as one writer put it, the government attempted to "legislate morality"—in Boston was rife with corruption, like any major city across America during that same period. Look, when you place a permanent ban on the sale, transportation, importation, and exportation of all alcoholic beverages, you drive the demand and the price of the product through the roof. The mobs were experts at exploiting this move by the fat cats in Washington and using it to expand their businesses. Still, the Prohibition Era was also a time of great expansion and growth for a city that had been the setting for the birth of a nation as shots were fired at Bunker Hill and the War for Independence broke out.

With Buccola's and Lombardo's gang in the driver's seat, was there a better place to expand the Italian side of the Mafia, who were quickly taking over leadership roles throughout New England in Providence, Hartford, and even as far south as New York City? Some have said Phil Buccola took over in Boston after Gaspare Messina, who had inherited the godfather chair in the 1920s, died in 1924, while others swore Messina was ruling the Boston-based side of the business well into the 1930s. This part of the history of the Boston Mob is a bit tricky to wade through. Yet, as one writer said years later, Buccola, coming into power in 1932, was a better fit. He had the "recognition as Boston boss [during that time] from the national Mafia commission." And the relationship between Buccola and Lombardo had always been something of folklore and mystery. There are claims that Lombardo was Buccola's underboss and that Lombardo ruled one side of the city and Buccola the other. Vincent Teresa, who became one of the most infamous stoolies on record, maintained that Joey Lombardo was the boss of the city during those days.

Whatever the case may be, Phil Buccola was one of those traditional Sicilian Mafioso who came to the United States in 1920 amid a wave of criminal migration, a time when wiseguys from Italy were running from the law in the motherland. This was when Buccola entered the country as a fighting promoter. After being in Beantown for a time, Buccola saw there was much more money to be made on the streets than in the ring, and there was even a good chance he could juxtapose the two within the crime world, fixing fights at will. Buccola's first gang hailed from the East Side, an honest-to-goodness, traditional, knuckle-busting, leg-breaking crew of Sicilians who believed the best way to send a message about an unpaid bill was through violence—the more brutal, the better. The popular term La Cosa Nostra ("this thing of ours") came from that Mafia mentality brought over from Sicily, branding Sicilians with a reputation for being the most ruthless, heartless, and bloody mobsters on the planet. And it was not only the bloodshed in their wake and fear of violence the mob put into people that built the Sicilians up as the most feared; it was the way in which they ran the business: "During the twentieth century," investigative reporter Clarence Walker writes in *American Mafia*, "the powerful rise of the Sicilian mafia grew into a booming business. They controlled most of the country's economic resources: land, agriculture, estates, manufactured goods, and even served as mediators for peasants, landowners, and foreign traders. Sicilian mafia dominance was so fearful even the police asked permission to travel into certain areas of the islands, particularly in Palermo, a breeding ground for notorious mob bosses." And this dynamic, as more and more Mafioso made the overseas trip from the home country to Boston, ended up on the streets of Beantown.

Palermo Sicilians were the group who came up with that familiar Mafia hierarchy—based in part on the way in which an army worked—that we all know today (the Mafia tree or chart): At the top of the pyramid is your *cupola* (board of directors); then you have your *caporegime* (those individual bosses from each "family"); and finally, your fighting men, the soldiers, those "made" guys who ran the streets, banged heads, collected the vigs, shook down bar and store owners, and used various other strong-arm tactics, along with pouring the cement shoes of those men who didn't live up to their place in the the chain. If one wants an example of a Palermo-based, Sicilian Mafia family made ultra-famous by Hollywood, he or she would have to look no further than the Corleone family, brought to life by Mario Puzo in his book *The Godfather.* As Puzo wrote of the Mafia oath, the Sicilian law of *omerta* (silence among men), "Blood was blood and nothing was its equal."

In Boston, this fictional code would prove to be true.

Not knowing the impact of the Gustin Gang murders when they occurred, twelve-year-old North End Beantown native Gennaro "Jerry" Angiulo, who had undoubtedly heard about the ambush as a child running the streets, eventually became the leader of the Boston Mafia. Buccola was a good face for the mob as it settled into its Italian run; but authors Brian Wallace and Bill Crowley explain in *Final Confession: The Unsolved Crimes of Phil Cresta,* "he often gave second and third chances to those who went against him." And any wiseguy worth the weight of his .38 knew you were only as good as your reputation. You could not have a softie running the operation. The organization as a whole would suffer and certainly be taken advantage of whenever the opportunity arose. The Italians had fought long and hard to take the action and the streets away from the Irish; it wouldn't take much to relinquish that ground they had worked so hard and so violently to master; and the Irish, fickle as they were, not to mention on the cusp of stepping back into the fray, were waiting for the right situation to take back what they believed had been theirs by blood, their firm roots in the community, and land ownership.

Angiulo was over two decades younger than Phil Buccola. He was a lot smarter and more inclined to look at the Mafia as a business rather than a leg-breaking team of hoods who took what they wanted and left a trail of blood. Lest we forget—and it should not be overlooked— Angiulo had three brothers who were with him all the way and, together, this crew broke many bones and put many men into early graves. Still, Angiulo understood how a business was supposed to run. Buccola and Lombardo, on the other hand, although not terribly old, were aging crooks. Angiulo saw this and realized a new breed of Mafioso needed to take control before the reign was lost forever back to the Irish.

"By 1961," authors O'Neill and Lehr write, "Angiulo and his four brothers were running the Boston Mafia and, by extension, much of the criminal activity in New England with a ruthless, and enormously profitable efficiency."

One cannot argue with success.

So how did Angiulo and his brothers achieve this task?

They turned to one man: Phil Cresta.

By Boston standards, Phil Cresta, a Boston native who grew up on the streets and knew the wiseguys who could help him with whatever he needed, had respect among his brethren, but also among his adversaries. Even more, he was fearless, willing to do anything. One afternoon in 1962, President John F. Kennedy was being inaugurated. Everyone in Boston was of course glued to the television as a hometown hero was placed into the nation's top position. As local patrons in a bar frequented by Cresta sat sipping brews and watching television, Cresta slipped outside and lifted three parking meters from city streets. He sat down at the bar with the meters in front of him and ordered a drink. Turning and looking, those sitting nearby laughed and laughed, slapping Cresta on the back, telling him what balls he had. But Cresta wasn't done. He took the meters home and eventually made keys to fit each model (the city used three different versions then for this very reason!). Now with keys in hand, he had several official meter-reading uniforms custom made for himself and his mates. Over the course of about fourteen months, Phil Cresta and his cronies stole close to $100,000 in meter money.

In the end, though, Cresta would fall to the failures of the Angiulo business model. "Angiulo never learned the value of loyalty and never had the restraint of true leadership," O'Neill and Lehr write. "It . . . hurt him in the end."

All told, Cresta was a prolific thief and heist artist. He was able to steal millions of dollars' worth of jewels, art, and cash. He was able to take the Boston Mafia and move it into a new era of criminals as the conservative 1950s gave way to the more liberal 1960s, when the FBI stepped into the fray and became engrained in Boston politics and crime. By this time, Buccola had retired to Sicily and the Providence faction of the New England mob was stronger than it had even been. And while Phil Cresta, Angiulo, and another merciless mobster, Raymond Patriarca ("fair but ferocious . . . when crossed," who took control in 1954 of both Providence and Boston), were on top, the Irish were building up their fleet, gang by gang, street by street, fight by fight. Internal issues and small town pride, however, would ultimately stifle any serious progress made by the Irish, who were all set to give the Italians a run—and once again, as history had foretold, there would be bloodshed before a handing over of the torch could take place.

~~~

It all started over a girl.

Labor Day weekend. The fall of 1961. As it stood, there were two main Irish mobs who, radio host Howie Carr writes in *The Brothers Bulger,* "coexisted relatively peacefully" for quite a long time as they entertained business in the neighboring Boston towns of Somerville and Charlestown. The streets were gritty back then. Bostonians of all kinds, Boston Bruins hockey fans and Red Sox diehards, walked the blocks alongside Irish mobsters and their cronies. Everyone knew one another's place. Crime was a part of life. You had your shakedowns and burglaries. You saw your share of beatings and drunken arguments over money and street turf. Bloodshed was something you understood as part of the mob culture. But you never, beyond reason, opened your mouth about any of it. If you lived in this section of Boston and knew anyone with Celtic blood running through his veins, red hair and freckles or not, you kept to yourself, zipped your lips, and went about your business.

The Winter Hill Gang ran Somerville. The boss then was James "Buddy" McLean, a slicked-back, black-haired, clean-cut scrub with sharp eyes and thin lips. The one quotation that fits McLean probably better than any other, aptly orated by an old partner of his, goes something like this: "He looks like a choir boy but fights like the Devil." As they say in Beantown ... *McLean was a wicked pisser with balls the size of cantaloupes.* The guy was willing to do whatever it took to get the job done.

Exactly what the Irish needed at the time.

On that Labor Day weekend when Patsy Cline and Roy Orbison would have been ruling the airwaves at Salisbury Beach, a pristine slice of Massachusetts/New Hampshire shoreline landscape, everyone enjoying the last blast of the summer, a couple of Winter Hill Gang members were hanging out at a rented cottage along the coastline. One was grocer Bill Hickey, an Irish mobster. Hickey and his partner were hanging with their girlfriends and another wiseguy, George McLaughlin, who was a soldier in the Somerville crew run by his brother, Bernie McLaughlin. The gangs were generally cordial to each other, understanding that bad blood between them would hurt business and not do anybody any good.

According to how the Winter Hill boys later reported it, George had one too many drinks that day and became belligerent and physical, touchy-feely, with Bill Hickey's girlfriend. During one of his drunken escapades, George groped the breast of Hickey's girl.

Big mistake.

"Hey," Hickey raged.

Another guy, a roofer named Red Lloyd, encouraged George to end it there: "You need to apologize to the lady."

George refused.

Pride and ego—a poisonous mixture in these types of bad boys.

Hickey became furious and went after George in a fit of rage. George was totally inebriated and couldn't defend himself. At one point, Lloyd got between them, trying to break up the fight by offering the two of them a glass of whiskey.

George took the glass, downed the alcohol, and smashed the glass into Lloyd's face, busting him up pretty good, spewing blood all over the place.

That was it. According to one source, Hickey and Lloyd gave George "the beating of his life." In fact, Lloyd, seemingly unfazed by the whiskey glass broken over his face, proceeded to knock George out cold—and then the two of them pummeled the mobster, kicking and walloping his limp body until they believed he was dead.

After realizing George was still alive, Lloyd and Hickey carried him to their car and dropped him off on the front lawn of a local emergency room. Then they hightailed it back to Somerville to find their leader, Buddy McLean.

The boss was not going to like what he was about to be told.

Those brass balls of Buddy's, well, let's just say that he was going to have to shine them up a bit, because there was definitely going to be a price to pay for George's beating. After all, George spent a month in the hospital. His brother, Bernie, after picking George up and driving him home, went over to see Buddy.

"Those two need to be dead, Buddy. I need you to set them up."

Bernie was talking about Lloyd and Hickey, of course.

This was a test for Buddy. A line had been drawn on the street. Should he cave in to the demands of rival Mafioso or tell him to F off?

"You *need* to set them up," Bernie reiterated.

"No way," Buddy said firmly.

Bernie didn't argue. Or even wait for a response. He stormed out of the house.

Buddy was awoken that night by barking dogs. They were trying to tell him that something was going on outside.

"What's going on?" Buddy said to the canines as he forced himself out of bed and over to the window. "What is it?"

Staring outside, Buddy spied two men doing something to his car. So he got dressed, grabbed his gun, kicked the door open, and began firing into the air.

This scared the men off.

Still armed and on guard, Buddy walked out to his car and looked under the hood, where he had seen the men congregating.

There it was: Dynamite. Bernie McLaughlin had rigged Buddy's vehicle to explode.

It was game on. Buddy McLean couldn't allow such a breach of trust between the two rival gangs to go without retaliation. He was now stuck in the middle: Respond and deal with the consequences, or turn away and be seen as pushover, and maybe even lose his spot.

The following day, which happened to be Halloween, Buddy took a detour through downtown Charlestown after a court appearance. He knew Bernie McLaughlin liked to sit in front of the Morning Glory Lounge (insert an image here of Tony Soprano and the boys hanging out in front of Satriale's Pork Store, sipping espressos and smoking cigars, and you get the picture). And sure enough, Bernie was there, sitting, talking to his boys.

It was noon. There were a reported one hundred or more people in the square on that afternoon, dozens more standing near Bernie. Buddy walked up calmly behind Bernie, without saying a word, and, in front of about twenty people, put a cap in the back of Bernie's fat head.

Bernie dropped like a bag of sand. Dead. And never knew what hit him.

For his deed, Buddy McLean went to jail for two years on a weapons charge—none of the witnesses in the square that day would testify against him.

Nobody dun seen nuttin'.

As Howie Carr put it in his book about the Bulger brothers, with this one hit, "The war was on, and before it was over, more than forty Boston hoodlums would be dead."

⌁

That bar fight in Hampton Beach had set in motion several important and critical consequences in the development and history of the Boston Mafia. For one, when the war started, the Italians, for the most part, stood by and watched their adversaries and competition kill one another, day in and day out. As Andy Metzger put it in his article about the Somerville–Winter Hill Gang fight that escalated into bloodshed the likes of which Boston had never seen, "The murder sparked a war that would leave [scores of] people dead, culminating with the gunning down of [Buddy] McLean, on Broadway. Local bookies were taking bets on how long McLean . . . and other Winter Hill notables would survive, and the men lived in safe-houses away from their families."

Public and media attention to what became massive bloodshed and violence and arrests on the streets of Boston began to affect all aspects of the Mafia. It was not good for anyone. Within ten years, the Charlestown Mob fizzled into nothing, with any surviving members realizing that all they could do was either join the Winter Hill Gang or die. After all, they were all Irish. Why not form one united super group of headknockers and become almighty powerful? Fighting each other was not only a losing proposition; it was stupid.

With its leaders dead or in prison, and Buddy McLean now buried six feet under, the stage was set for another new crop of wiseguys, a breed of mobsters that would soon rival the Italians.

"The remnants of the Charlestown Mob were then absorbed into the Winter Hill Gang, who were then able to become the dominant Irish Mob in the New England area," reported an article.*

It was 1972, a year in what was truly an American era for the history books. Watergate. Hank Aaron became the first baseball player to sign for—get this!—$200,000 a year. John and Yoko were told to get the hell out of the country. Bruce Springsteen signed his first record deal. M*A*S*H premiered on television. *Life* magazine published its final edition. In the midst of all this, the Winter Hill Gang had just taken over control of East Boston and was on its way to becoming one of the most "successful organized crime groups in American history"—a reign of criminality that would continue for decades and take on new form in the coming years, when one of the most infamous names in American Mafia lore stepped out from behind a curtain and onto the playing field as a leader of the Winter Hill Gang.

James J. "Whitey" Bulger.

～

With the rise of Bulger and Steven "Rifleman" Flemmi during the late 1970s came a fresh business model for the Boston Mafia. No more was it about simply breaking heads and shaking down

---

* No byline given, "An Offer You Can't Refuse: Organized Crime in Major American Cities." Virginia.edu

people for chump change, stealing meter money or hijacking bottles of booze from trucks and ships. Sure, they still committed these crimes; but with the likes of Flemmi and Bulger at the helm, old-school violence and racketeering were replaced by a renewed sense of entitlement, a gruesome, brutal strategy many had not been accustomed to. Bookmaking became one of Bulger's main sources of income, and, as this puny, squeaky Irish man developed a reputation within an area of Boston known as Southie for supposedly keeping the blacks and their drugs out of the projects by strong-arming them, Bulger and his gang were one of the major suppliers, giving Southie notoriety as the cocaine capital of the city.

In order to place himself in a position where he was one of Boston's Mafia leaders, some say Bulger murdered sixteen men on his way up that ladder, including his former boss, Don Killeen, and other rival gang members. Bulger also infiltrated the FBI, becoming an informant, ratting out his Italian counterparts and, more importantly, cultivating FBI sources that were about to help him take total control of the Southie streets like no one ever had.

Those neighborhoods in Southie are some of the most notorious and infamous Boston has to offer. As Michael Patrick McDonald writes in *All Souls,* his book about growing up in Southie, "I . . . saw the junkies, the depressed, and lonely mothers of people who died, the wounded, the drug dealers, and a known murderer accepted by everyone as warmly as they accepted anyone." Whitey Bulger is likely that pleasant and likable "murderer" McDonald refers to in this passage about the Old Harbor Housing project, formally the Mary Ellen McCormack Project, just opposite the Carson Beach area, where McDonald spent his youth. Throughout the years, in this blue-collar, welfare-poor section of Boston run by the Irish, Bulger has been, the *New York Times* reported, "a modern-day Robin Hood or a ruthless killer, depending on whom you ask." Some refer to Whitey as a legend, a man who helped people and took care of those in the neighborhood who didn't have a pot to piss in. "No one made us feel better about where we lived than Whitey Bulger," McDonald writes. Whitey was a folk hero to the working class, welfare mothers, and Irish immigrants living in Southie (at a time when some were even questioning Whitey's Irish roots). He was viewed as a patriarch and "good brother," a man who gave back to the community and protected it from the thugs in other neighborhoods.

Whitey Bulger was arrested in 1956 for robbing several banks in Massachusetts, Rhode Island, and Indiana. Caught, he did nine years in federal prison, three at the infamous Alcatraz off the coast of San Francisco. While Whitey was gone doing his time, the perfect situation was setting itself up in Southie and East Boston, allowing this crook and mobster to walk out of prison and literally take over. Howie Winter had taken over for Buddy McLean after Buddy's demise in 1965. Winter had always been considered what they called a "non-Mafia" gangster (he did the same things, broke the same heads, but officially ran with no particular gang). But after a run in with the McLaughlin boys, who blew up Howie's car in 1962, Winter decided to get into the ring officially. He met with Ray Patriarca in Providence and explained to the New England mob leader a plan for setting up in Southie. Soon, Winter was operating out of a garage on Marshall Street in Somerville, with a seat at Chandler's Bar in Southie. Whitey joined forces with Winter after Whitey knocked off Don Killeen, a local gangster/wiseguy who had, up until then, run certain sections of Southie. And then slowly—even methodically, perhaps—Whitey took over for Winter after Winter was pinched for several different schemes, including a pinball extortion racket and horse race fixing system he had developed and implemented. Winter and his band of gangsters were busted and run off the streets of Southie. Most wound up in prison or dead. This opened the door wide for Whitey and his main henchman, Flemmi, to step in and take control.

Funny that nobody back then asked the one obvious question: Why weren't Bulger and Flemmi hauled in and brought up on charges, too? Seemed the entire South Boston mob was being handcuffed, perp-walked out of bars and home, and sent away. How had Bulger and his men escaped the law?

Bulger and Flemmi would have been swept up under that same umbrella of arrests that nabbed Winter and his crew, but Whitey had been paying off FBI agents, while developing intelligence for later blackmail schemes on certain agents who were helping him. Whitey Bulger had the FBI in his back pocket. As the *Times* reported, "Bulger [was] the organized crime boss who always gets away. Whenever the police placed wiretaps at what they identified as his loan-sharking headquarters, he seemed to learn about it the same day and change locations."

And for about twenty years this system worked for Bulger. The Justice Department eventually indicted and convicted just about every other mob leader in New England as Whitey looked on from the sidelines, escaping the shackles of justice time and again.

But then the day finally came when the feds busted Whitey's FBI sources and the curtain seemingly closed on Southie's balding, skinny, white-haired savior. It was January 1995. Word on the street was that Bulger was going to be indicted by a Federal grand jury in Boston on charges of racketeering and extortion. This was, of course, only the beginning. After he was taken in, Bulger was set to face multiple charges of murder. In the interim, it was uncovered that one of the FBI agents Bulger had been using as his inside source was providing information to Bulger's crew that they used to kill rivals and others.

A few days before the grand jury handed down that indictment on Bulger, however, someone tipped old Whitey off, which gave him the opportunity to disappear.

While Whitey was out on the run, the FBI admitted that he had been a confidential government informer for nearly twenty years: from 1971 to 1990. Imagine: Nineteen years of giving up his Italian adversaries—and likely a few of his own—to cover his own ass. If it had been known at any time during that period, Bulger would have been cut into little pieces and tossed into Boston Harbor as flounder bait.

Rumors swirled for sixteen years—and the Bulger name became as infamous as Hoffa. There were stories of Bulger living large in an FBI camp somewhere in Middle America, sipping Irish whiskey and smoking Cubans, betting on the ponies. Some claimed the FBI put a bullet in Bulger's head and ground up his body because of all he knew about scores of rogue FBI agents. And there were even more stories so incredible, they seem too erroneous to repeat here. Truth be told, however, Whitey ended up on the FBI's 10 Most Wanted list, facing charges in nineteen murders, above and beyond a host of other charges under the indictment. The real story was that Bulger was not dead or holed up somewhere living off federal FBI money; he was on the run, possibly with a new face via plastic surgery and an alias that had served him for nearly two decades. And then the FBI, who had a bit of a sour taste in its mouth from this situation (to say the least), got smart. They knew Bulger had taken off with a woman, Catherine Greig, and that putting out a $2 million reward for information leading to where Whitey was hiding out had probably been a futile effort. Ratting out the mob boss who was known to have once strangled a woman while carrying her down the stairs of a three-decker and had beaten and tortured a man so badly that he actually asked Whitey to put a bullet in his head was not a good idea and not likely to happen.

So the FBI decided to focus on Whitey's companion, Greig. First, the agency doubled the reward (from $50,000 to $100,000) for information leading to the capture of Greig. Second, the FBI began to place ads on television shows such as Dr. Oz, which are known to be viewed mostly by females, and even bought full-page ads in *Plastic Surgery News* and the American Dental Association newsletter, posting a photo of Greig while pleading with readers: "Have you treated this woman?"

For years the FBI had nothing to go on but leads that led to dead ends.

But then it paid off . . . finally.

In late June 2011, sixteen years after Bulger and Greig took off, a courageous source called in a tip that led the FBI to a home in Santa Monica, California, which ended an international manhunt for a man who was thought to be dead by this point. And yet there he was, eighty-one-year-old Whitey Bulger, looking older and frailer then he ever had, certainly with whiter hair and a beard and glasses, living amid a community of middle-class suburbanites in sunny Cali, Catherine Greig and about $800,000 in cash by his side.

Greig, a sixty-year-old dental hygienist who'd had multiple plastic surgeries and reportedly had her teeth whitened and cleaned once a month, was arrested with Bulger and taken into custody. What happens now to Whitey Bulger, whether he begins to sing and turn over names of FBI agents, whether he gives up other mob bosses, whether he keeps his mouth shut and fights the charges, is inconsequential to the fact that the man has been brought in. And if anyone thought the FBI had even stopped looking, or did not want to find Bulger because of what he could possibly say about the agency, Special Agent Richard Teahan, who led the Boston task force searching for Bulger all those years, put it best when he told the *Times:* "There is absolutely no fatigue factor whatsoever."

A Brief Note from the Author

Before you begin this next trio of stories, I want to point out that they are quite a bit longer than the previous five in this collection. The stories that follow are more contemporary, so it was easier for me to obtain an abundance of research, conduct interviews with some of the players involved, and dig deeper into the characters and facts of the cases. I have reported on these stories for many years and even written about them in various forms, but for whatever reason, I never turned any of them into feature-length true-crime books.

The murders you have read about in this collection up to this point have a sense of gruesomeness and brutality within them found throughout history, but, in a sense, we are almost able to detach ourselves from them because the murders happened so long ago. There's this subtle feeling in some of the previous stories that the murders did not happen at all; the historical element of each allows us to think of them as folklore or campfire tales handed down throughout the centuries.

That said, in the stories that follow, I am certain you will feel these murders as if they had taken place on your block or in your immediate neighborhood—or maybe even to a family member. The sheer sociopathic nature involved in these next three crimes—the idea that the killers just didn't give two bits about human life—is inevitable and apparent. It will shock and astound you, same as it did for me as I researched and reported on them.

I hope there are lessons we can take from each story here and apply to our lives. I have my own opinions and thoughts about what we can learn from each of the true-crime stories that follow, but I'll keep those to myself (except for one, that is, which you will run into at the end) and let you, the reader, take out of each what you can.

Lastly, before you begin reading, I want to pay mind to something important to me: My thoughts, prayers, condolences, and sympathies are with the families of these murder victims.

CHAPTER 6

Electronic Kill Machine

Summer 2001: Norton, Massachusetts

Eighteen-year-old Jim Morel was out jogging one afternoon, not long after the ordeal he had gone through with his childhood friends was over. Murder. Jim was running in the country air of Massachusetts, trying to clear his head. He was thinking about the future. Jim had turned on his friends, some would say. He was a rat, others would proclaim. He was a hero, still others would argue. Either way, Jim wanted to forget about the past year and move on with his life.

As he jogged in a secluded area in Norton, Massachusetts, a "big blue car," Jim later described, pulled up behind him, caught up, and then stopped.

This got Jim's attention. He had been looking over his shoulder lately.

"Are you Jim Morel?" one of the two guys in the car asked. They were hulking men, big and brawny, Jim noticed as they got out and approached him. Jim had never seen them before.

"Yeah, yeah . . . why? What's up?" Jim was sweating. Out of breath.

Jim thought maybe they were old friends. *Grammar school? Junior high?* It was getting late in the day, darker. Dusk. He couldn't really make out their faces.

According to Jim, however, these men were not there to reminisce about the glory days—they were there to hurt him.

Hurt him bad.

One of the guys, Jim said, ran toward him with a "kitchen knife" and started stabbing into the air before hitting Jim in the arm.

"What the heck are you—" Jim said. He had no idea what was happening—but he knew why.

Before Jim could say anything else, the guy with the knife went for Jim's face and started slashing.

Feeling the warm trickle of blood running down his cheeks and arm, Jim took off as fast as he could into the nearby woods, literally running for his life.

❦

They had a name that was hardcore. A lot to swallow if you didn't "get it": *Electronic Kill Machine.* But then, "hardcore" described this group of teens who made up the band and the posse hanging around to watch rehearsals and attend gigs.

Jim Morel was seventeen then. It was long before he was viciously attacked that Sunday evening while out jogging. Jim played keyboards. He had a clean-cut appearance: light hair, skinny, tall, baby face. He wasn't some head banger who walked around with a chain hanging from his ear to his nose, tattoos, studded bracelets, ripped jeans, black Harley boots, metal dotted about his face. Jim just loved the music. For him, it was all about the music.

"That band was a cross between electronic and, like, a heavier rock," Jim said, "but it was more abstract, kind of dark."

Old-school Marilyn Manson meets a contemporary SlipKnot, in other words.

That darkness Jim associated with the music had also infected the lives of some of Electronic Kill Machine's members—especially the drummer, Jason Weir. Thomas Lally and Anthony Calabro, along with Weir, were kids Jim had grown up with in Norton. As friends go, they were tight.

"Ant"—as Anthony Calabro was called by his crew, Weir and Lally—Jim said, loved nothing more than "getting high and watching hours upon hours of *Forensic Files.*"

They lived in Quincy. They liked to sit around and drink and smoke weed and watch hours of the show, intrigued by the mere stupidity of some criminals.

"It got to the point where they were actually taking down notes," Jim recalled.

They not only watched the show and other forensic crime shows like it, but they'd go online afterward and study each of the cases like students. They'd pull up witness statements and photographs and court files and dissect each case as if it were some sort of high school assignment.

"Towards the end," Jim recalled, "they were just *obsessed* with the show."

It got to the point where Lally, Ant, and Weir looked at Jim and other kids in the group and, with smiles on their faces, said things as bizarre as, "We could kill somebody and get away with it."

Jim and the others would shake it off, maybe have a laugh.

Yeah, right. You guys—killers? No way.

❦

The neighborhood Jim Morel and his buddies—Lally, Weir, and Ant Calabro—grew up in forty miles south of Boston, in and around Norton, was not so much rough as it was working-class. Norton, Brockton, Foxboro (home of the New England Patriots), Canton; these towns are suburbs, outside the confines of places like Quincy, Brookline, and Chelsea, where the streets are a little more hardscrabble and rough.

Still, for Jim and his friends, living amid white picket fences and lawn mowers and cul-de-sacs didn't change things at home. "We all kind of came from broken homes," Jim remembered. "We all kind of, like, moved in together and became each other's families."

It was the summer of 2001, as Jim told it. Ant was eighteen then. Lally twenty-one. Weir, like Jim, the youngest at seventeen. Jason was talented, Jim claimed. A solid drummer. Lally just hung around with the band, one of those wannabes or groupies. And Ant, well, Anthony Calabro was the band's self-proclaimed "manager." He was the kid who was going to take the group over the top, to the next level, get them a record deal.

Ant lived with his great aunt, eighty-four-year-old Marina Calabro. Marina owned a triplex, a large three-decker in Quincy. Marina and Ant lived on the third floor. Weir and Lally soon moved in after leaving home and having nowhere to go and no one to turn to. Ant loved his great aunt. Jim said he talked about her a lot. How kind and gentle, how outgoing the old woman had been.

Marina agreed to allow the kids to live with her. After all, she had a lot of money stowed away, and owned property worth some serious coin.

"Whatever Ant needed, she bought it for him," Jim said. Ant crashed a car once. Marina stepped in and bought him a new one, then paid for his insurance, too. "I don't remember Ant ever having to work. Most of us had jobs. He didn't. She just paid for everything."

Marina adored Ant to the point of telling him that she was willing her entire estate—everything she owned, near $1.2 million—to him. Ant was sitting on a hefty inheritance. He was young. Even if Marina lived to be ninety-four years old, it would only be ten years until then.

Jim Morel and his three buddies were recluses: They didn't travel much beyond the comfort zone of their own group and neighborhood. They didn't really make new friends. Jim's friend, Jason Weir, was a pretty bright kid, Jim recalled. "He, like the rest of us, came from a broken family. He'd done his fair share—like all of us—of crimes, but nothing too major."

They'd all been busted with drugs or in trouble for one reason or another. It was part of being a teen in suburban Boston and not having much direction or drive in life.

"The cops knew all our names," Jim said. "I was by no means an angel."

Jim went to high school with Thomas Lally. They were in a special program. They didn't go to classes with the other kids. There were a certain number of "troubled" kids, Jim admitted, who attended classes in the basement of the school. Out of the entire group, Lally was the first of the bunch to take things to a severely extreme level. Ant would soon take the title from Lally. But in high school and even right after, Lally was known as the "crazy kid" who would do just about anything.

"He was very obsessed with, like, explosives," Jim remembered.

Lally liked to wear army fatigues and was into blowing things up for fun.

"He was odd. He did a lot of bizarre things."

Lally suffered from Tourette syndrome, which, according to the National Institute of Neurological Disorders and Stroke, is "a neurological disorder characterized by repetitive, stereotyped, involuntary movements and vocalizations called tics." People with Tourette will often shout obscenities uncontrollably and experience violent body twitching and sharp jerks of the arms and shoulders and head.

This made Lally stand out.

For anyone who suffers from the disorder, it's a debilitating condition. Lally was a big guy back then: over six feet tall and at least 250 pounds. Not too many people screwed with Lally or questioned the bizarre behavior brought on by the Tourette. His profile would shrink later, but back when the Norton gang ran together, Lally was the monster of the clan.

"He blew up a dog house once, it was wild," Jim explained. "We had, like, grenade launchers and stuff like that. Where other kids might have had, like, 9 mms and .38s, we had *bombs*."

—⁓—

Lally, Jason, and Ant became so obsessed with *Forensic Files* that they were now sitting around the Quincy apartment they shared during the summer of 2000 into 2001 discussing the various ways in which they could kill someone and get away with it. It became like a game: Smoke some weed and then come up with the best scenario you could to kill a person and walk away a free man.

"They would talk about chemicals," Jim said. "How they could dip their fingers in certain chemicals and acids and it wouldn't destroy certain pieces of their fingers, but it would take off any fingerprints."

They also talked about the best way to commit the murder. For example, what would be the chosen weapon—the most sensible—with which to kill someone?

Not a gun, obviously, which, according to them, would leave a path for authorities to track down the perp—aka, trace evidence.

A knife would leave the same.

Strangulation or asphyxiation?

No. Hand prints could be matched up to bruises.

But an accident . . . yes! That was it, the threesome decided. To murder someone and get away with it, the best way would be to make it look like an accident.

Stage the scene.

It seemed evil to break murder down to such a strategic way of thinking, but how many murders were committed where the killers didn't follow a few simple rules? Every crime show had made this point at one time or another. And Lally, Weir, and Ant, often stoned out of their minds, had figured this out while watching *Forensic Files*. On certain nights, in fact, perhaps when boredom overcame the value of good drugs, they'd act out certain crimes. Jim Morel said he'd show up at the apartment Ant lived in with Marina, Lally, and Weir, and they'd be sitting around—bong on the table—discussing how to do it right.

"Hit a person this way and it would work."

"It would! Yes."

They dissected murders to the point where they believed the best way to understand the perfect murder was to look at it backwards. Take the result—in other words—and walk through backwards to see how to do it perfectly and without making one mistake. It took only one mishap and you were caught, the three of them knew by watching television. Every murderer in prison made that one mistake—oftentimes it was something simple—that pointed police in his direction.

They talked about it over and over, night after night—and then . . . well, and then they came up with it.

A faultless plan.

"A frying pan," one of them said.

"A frying pan wrapped in a towel," another added.

Yes!

That's it.

Marina Calabro had recently retired from her hairdressing job. She was a sharp woman, not some docile old lady ready for a walker with tennis balls guiding the legs down the waxed hallway of a convalescent home. Marina cooked dinner and washed clothes and watched television and made Ant and his friends' beds every day. For some reason, she had never married. She had no children—which was probably one of the reasons she took Ant into her home, along with his two friends, and treated Ant as her own.

Many claimed that Ant, as time went on, started to despise the woman for some reason. When Marina was away, her house became a party zone—Ant and Lally and Weir the hosts.

Ant, like the other two, was a professional slacker. They were pot-smoking, alcohol-drinking kids who thought they had all the answers. They played video games all day long. Watched television. Ate McDonald's. Hung out at the local mall.

None of them wanted to work.

Marina put up with it. She might have expressed her feelings from time to time. But she allowed the behavior to continue.

Margaret Menz had known Ant for quite some time. She and Ant often traded stories when they ran into each other in the hallway of the three-decker, or outside in the driveway. During the afternoon of December 19, 2001, Menz left work early and returned home to that same building Marina shared with Ant and his buddies.

As Menz came up the street, oh, maybe three o'clock or so, she recalled later, she spied Ant sitting in Lally's truck outside the building in the driveway. Ant had his dog with him. The door to the truck was open. Ant seemed nervous. Not himself.

"Hey," Margaret said.

This startled Ant. He hadn't expected Menz to come home, obviously.

"Hey," Ant said, surprised to see her.

"What are you doin' sitting here in your truck?"

"I'm nervous," Ant said. "I got into an accident with my car."

Ant had totaled the car Marina had bought him and, he said, he didn't know how to go upstairs and tell her. She was going to be livid. She had purchased the ride for him and here he had gone and totally destroyed the thing.

After ten minutes of what Menz later called "small talk," she and Ant walked into the building from the backyard. As they made their way to the door to get into the building itself, Ant said, "You see that?"

"What?"

He pointed to his dog. "My dog senses something," Ant added.

It was an off-the-wall comment. Menz didn't know what to make of it.

As she and Ant approached the second level of the house from the back stairs, Menz asked Ant, "Is Marina in there?"

Ant had heard Menz's question and understood it, because he looked toward her after she asked, but did not answer. Instead, Ant walked into his second-story apartment without saying anything, and then closed the door.

Menz thought this was strange. Ant was not acting like himself. Something was different about him.

By 3:40 p.m. that same day, Menz left her apartment to meet up with her boyfriend. That truck Ant had been sitting in earlier when she arrived, Menz remembered, was still in the driveway when she walked out of the yard and down the block.

About 10:45 that night, after returning home from dinner, Menz heard a commotion in Marina's apartment. The walls and floors were paper thin. She didn't have much trouble making out what Ant said (she lived directly below), but couldn't believe what she was hearing.

"Dead . . . go home," Menz heard Ant mutter.

Dead, go home?

What did it mean?

It was near midnight on that same somber night when the Quincy Police Department (QPD) received a call from Ant. Marina had fallen down the stairs—at least that's what it looked like. Perhaps she had tried to carry a bag of trash down the narrow, steep flight of stairs inside the three-decker and somehow tripped? Perhaps she'd had a stroke? Maybe a heart attack?

Being in her mid-eighties, the fall had been too much on Marina's fragile body—according to Ant, she was dead.

Ant explained to the police that he and Thomas Lally had found Marina at the base of the stairs when they came home. Ant couldn't believe it. He was beyond upset, those who knew him later confirmed. He walked around in a daze during those days that followed. His great aunt, the one woman who had rescued him from the streets and his broken home, had fallen and died. He hadn't been there to stop it. He hadn't been there to help Marina when she needed him most. He was upset with himself.

Menz hadn't thought much of the *Dead . . . go home* comment she had heard through the floor. It could have been anything, after all. Maybe Ant had been watching television or horsing around with his buddies. Who the hell knew? But that all changed near midnight, an hour after Ant called police, when Menz got a phone call from another Calabro relative living in the same building on the first floor.

"Marina's dead," the relative explained.

"What?"

"There's blood everywhere . . ." the woman was hysterical.

"Someone'll be right there."

Margaret woke up her boyfriend. He rushed out of the house and down the stairs. Menz didn't want to look.

A minute later, he was back: "It looks like Marina fell down the stairs."

Menz sensed something was wrong. As her boyfriend described the scene, she thought, *That's odd; Marina is always so extremely careful going up and down the stairs.*

It was close to the midnight hour when cops arrived at Marina's Quincy three-decker. There, at the bottom of the interior stairs, was the badly bruised and twisted body of Marina Calabro, Ant's eighty-four-year-old great aunt. She looked terrible. Like she had not only fallen, but maybe been run over by a truck, too.

People were mingling about outside.

"What's going on?" someone asked.

Ant had called in Marina's death. Thomas Lally was with him. One of the cops on the scene noticed that Lally had fresh scratches on his face and what appeared to be a bite mark on his forearm.

"What's that from?" the cop asked.

"We were horsing around," Lally explained, "Me and Anthony. We got a little rough and fought last night."

The cop bought it.

Ant and Lally said they had returned home after a night out only to find Marina at the bottom of the stairs. It was horrible. They were both very upset.

Two police officers sat with Ant in the kitchen while another cop walked Lally into the living room. They were asked to explain what happened more than simply "we went out." Step by step. Hour by hour. The cops wanted to know what the two young men had done that night.

"I last saw Marina about three o'clock," Ant told police. "She was inside the apartment. Tom [Lally] was here."

The cop took notes. Ant kept looking into the living room as another officer questioned Lally.

"Was she on any medications or anything?"

"No," Anthony said.

"How was she feeling?"

"As far as I know, pretty good."

"What'd you and Mr. Lally do today?"

"We left about three and, in Tom's truck, took a ride over to the Emerald Square Mall. I drove."

"Why?"

"Tom's license is suspended."

"What did you buy at the mall?"

"We went there to get some more minutes for my cell phone."

The apartment was clean. Tidy. Picked up. Marina was no neat freak, but she liked to keep her place sanitary, that's for sure. Nothing seemed out of place. Nothing was missing. From the looks of it, Marina had taken a misstep and fallen several flights of stairs to a painful death.

But the cops weren't satisfied with Ant's answers just yet. They wanted more.

Ant was asked again what time he and Lally got home.

"It was around ten thirty," he said. By routine, he and Lally entered the apartment the same way they exited: through the back stairs. "When we walked in, the kitchen and parlor lights were both on. The door to Marina's bedroom was closed. Nothing seemed unusual. You know."

Same as any other night.

There was a time difference, however—911 hadn't taken the call from Ant until 11:53 p.m. To that, Ant said, "We realized when we got home that we had forgotten to get cigarettes. So we went back out to the Seven-Eleven on Adams Street"—right around the corner—"and then stopped at Nick's Sub Shop," nearby, "to get a submarine sandwich."

"What time did you get back?"

"Oh, about 11:00. Tom watched television and I went to make my bed and saw that the blanket was gone." Ant said his bed hadn't been made, which was odd. "Marina usually makes the beds."

When Ant realized his bed wasn't made, he explained, he and Lally started looking for Marina. They felt something was wrong. So Ant said he called his grandmother downstairs to ask if she had seen Marina.

"I haven't heard from her," Ant's grandmother said.

"She's not here, either."

"She might be with some friends in New Hampshire."

Ant said he called his father in Plymouth next, who said, "I haven't seen her."

"Check the hallway," Anthony said his father told him.

Ant said he held the phone. "Tom," Ant called out, after telling his father to hold on, "check the hallway for Marina."

Tom returned. "She's at the bottom of the stairs."

◆━━◆

Lally sat in the living room and waited for Ant's interview to conclude before his turn to talk came. One little discrepancy, one tiny piece of the story that didn't juxtapose with Ant's and the jig was up: They would be heading downtown.

"We left around three and went to the Emerald Square Mall because Anthony had to fill his cell phone minutes," Lally began. "I was going to check on a job at Wal-Mart, but we left the mall instead."

Ant hadn't mentioned Wal-Mart.

"We stopped at several dealerships and looked at cars in the Attleboro area. We headed back to Quincy about nine but there was a lot a traffic for some reason."

All easy enough to check out.

"When did you guys return?" (Such an innocent, seemingly easy question—but one, for an investigator, that could tell a lot.)

"Around ten thirty."

"Did you notice anything in the apartment out of the ordinary?"

"No. The kitchen light was on and Marina's bedroom doors were closed."

"Did you guys stay home?"

"No. I forgot that I needed cigarettes, so we went out to the Seven-Eleven and then to Nick's Sub Shop."

Lally kept to the story pretty much word for word: the calls Ant had made, opening the door, seeing Marina at the bottom of the stairs. Lally, though, ladled on the emotion. He said he ran down the stairs and looked at Marina. "I touched her hand to see if she was okay. I ran back up the stairs and told Anthony. . . . We both started crying."

"Tell me about those scratches and the bites," the cop asked, looking at Lally's arm and face.

Lally looked down. "Oh, yeah . . . Anthony was drinking vodka right out of the bottle, he was pretty shitfaced. Marina asked me to get the bottle from him. When I grabbed the bottle, Ant grabbed me and pushed me and we argued, and Ant scratched me in the face and bit me on the arm. Here, look . . ." He showed the cop his arm. "See?"

Both police officers went back into the kitchen and asked Ant about the incident.

He confirmed Lally's story.

As one of the officers took a look at Marina's body, he observed many things. Marina was lying face-down on the bottom stairway. She was wearing a white shirt, green flex pants, black socks, white sneakers. Her left sneaker was torn and her ankles were crossed at the bottom.

It certainly appeared to be an accidental fall.

In front of Marina's face was a "small pool of blood . . . there were two cuts on her head and some blood under her fingernails."

Another officer, a trooper with the Massachusetts State Police (MSP), came over just then and pointed something out to the officer. There was "dust that had been removed from the hallway on both sides, which was consistent with a fall," the trooper later wrote. In other words, the hallway was dusty. The force and the air from Marina's "fall" had made an imprint on the floor much like, say, a book might make if you were to drop it on a dusty table. The air from the force of the book going down would push out the dust on all sides.

Another trooper photographed the scene and the coroner came and removed Marina's body.

After conducting a rather routine autopsy, the medical examiner uncovered nothing out of the ordinary. Marina had apparently fallen down several flights of stairs and, during the process of that violent tumble, sustained multiple injuries that all contributed to her death. Among those injuries noted on the report were "head and neck trauma, facial abrasions, lacerations of the scalp, cervical vertebrae fracture, soft tissue hemorrhage, chest and abdominal trauma, three right rib fractures, five left rib fractures, contusions of the back and extremity contusions. . . . The cause of her death was blunt neck trauma," said the report.

"[T]he manner of her death was ruled an accident."

Ant showed up at band practice to watch rehearsals the day after Marina was found dead. He seemed pretty much out of it, Jim Morel later recalled. Down and depressed. Not talking too much.

But nobody busted on him; Ant had lost someone he loved.

"It wasn't for very long," Jim added, "but at first he was very upset."

Everyone gathered around Ant and showed support. Even though, Jim said, "We all had our suspicions."

Suspicions . . . because for the past year or more, here were three friends bragging and carrying on about how they could pull off the perfect murder and, lo and behold, Marina had turned up dead. Coincidence? Self-fulfilling prophecy?

The thought occurred to Jim that Ant, Lally, and Weir had murdered Marina, but, "I knew these guys, grew up with them. . . . I couldn't believe that they would do something like that. It was all about the friends you had in high school: 'Oh, I'm a big tough guy.' But, you know, whenever it came down to it, where someone like Ant would actually get into a fight, whatever, he'd kind of, like, wuss out."

Talking tough among these three was the norm, Jim said. One time, they talked of opening up a hit man service. They spoke about murder as though it could become a hobby. But Jim Morel believed there was no way the "boys," as he called them, had the stomach or the guts to carry it out.

Over the course of the next few days (which would soon turn into months), Ant fell into himself even more. He wouldn't look at anyone. You know, make eye contact. He always came across as being depressed. Yet, a week after Marina's death, Ant was already spending that inheritance he received—and on the most bizarre things imaginable. He walked up to Jim Morel one day. "I want to do some investments with you and the band," Ant said.

"Huh?" Jim was stunned. ("He was grieving, I thought. Maybe this was his way of mourning the woman.")

The band had a few record labels sniffing around, but nothing had come through. Some cash to get the band's brand out there, maybe finance a tour, help with equipment, would certainly facilitate that dream of making it big.

And so a partnership was born.

Ant became more invested—financially and emotionally—in Electronic Kill Machine as time went by, as did many of Jim Morel's other childhood friends. In fact, the entire clan, Lally, Weir, Ant, and everyone around them, soon played a part in the band: promotions, producing, marketing, whatever. Ant was the bank, of course, because he had more money now than he knew what to do with. According to Jim, Ant wouldn't even take rent from the tenants at the three-decker. They were all living for free.

Then there were the vehicles. The hot rods and sports cars. The bling. The flashy clothes. The games. The wads of Ben Franklins rolled up in Ant's pocket as though he was some thug rapper starring in a music video. Ant was walking around flipping people money . . . *Here, entertain me.* One time, Ant went up to someone and said, "Here," tossing her a few hundred bucks, "make me smile."

Ant Calabro . . . Mr. Big Shot with all the dough.

According to Jim Morel, Ant was one of about five friends who were "networking out, you must understand: We created our own family atmosphere. Our own place. Our own ideals. Our own rules. And our own standards on everything. We became our *own* family. . . . We trusted each other with our lives. We weren't friends—we were brothers."

Margaret Menz was watching television one day not long after Marina had fallen down the stairs and died. Rumors were rampant that Ant had had something to do with Marina's death, but what could anyone do: The cops had investigated and closed the case. Officially speaking, Marina's death was a terrible accident.

As Menz watched television, she heard a ruckus outside her window. So she got up and went over to the window.

Looking down, Menz observed Ant smashing many of Marina's things—her old furniture and some knickknacks.

Strange, Menz thought, looking on.

Ant busted the stuff up and put the remains out with the rubbish.

That's so impersonal, Menz said to herself. Did the guy not have any respect for the woman's memory?

And then, as the days turned into weeks, the music and parties started inside Ant's portion of the three-decker. Ant and his friends started having get-togethers well into the night and the next day, yelling and screaming and throwing things out the windows. TVs. Radios. Beer bottles. Whatever.

They were living like rock stars.

All on Marina's money.

It was maybe a month after Marina's death. Jim Morel was hanging out a lot in Quincy at "the house," the three-decker Marina had left Ant. The apartment was in shambles: holes in the walls, empty bottles of booze everywhere, people sleeping here and there. A real-life animal house.

One morning near 3:00 a.m. there were about fifteen people in the apartment going crazy, drinking and smoking, blaring loud music, shouting like they didn't give a shit.

"We were all just singing this random song, chanting, loudly . . . singing . . . drunk out of our minds," Jim Morel recalled. "I remember thinking, God, the neighbors must *hate* us."

Jim mentioned something about it to Jason Weir.

"Who cares," Weir said. "They won't say anything. They live here for free. Ant doesn't even charge them rent, he just doesn't care."

Jim and Ant sat down to go over the business partnership they had entered into. "Believe it or not," Jim said, "Ant was intelligent. He knew percentages and business. He understood that the money he was giving me for the band was paying him back in a good profit."

The drugs and the alcohol were getting to Ant, however. He couldn't do much of anything anymore except deaden an obvious pain growing inside him. The question was, especially for Jim, *Where was all that pain coming from—Marina's death?*

The mourning was over. What was bothering Ant? What was he running from?

The money, Jim realized, gave Ant a sense of power. He felt as if he could buy anything he wanted. It wasn't unlike him to have $100,000 in cash hanging around the house. He knew that when the cash was gone, he could get at least another $500K for the house itself. If he needed it, what the hell, he'd sell the damn house.

Then Ant had an epiphany one day. He decided to start his own business.

"Mercenaries," Jim Morel said. "Yes, *mercenaries*. I thought it was completely, totally ridiculous."

Ant was about to put into action that dream he had always had about starting a professional hit man service.

Jim explained, "With the kind of guys, like, you see in the movies: Basically, you go there and you pay the guy and he comes in and he either really scares the person . . . or kills them, or whatever."

Ant approached Jim one day with a concept for the business, saying, "I want to open a website."

"Look," Jim told him, "I don't want anything to do with this, man. I think it's kind of, well, stupid."

"Okay."

Jim couldn't help but think that a professional contract killer, as Ant had said he wanted to be, would never open a website and announce his intentions.

"It just seemed like a really *stupid* idea." Then again, part of Jim thought—believed—Ant was just kidding. He was bored with life. He was rich, had anything he wanted. He needed something to keep him occupied.

Jim Morel began to believe that by killing Marina—and, like everyone else around them, Jim was now certain Ant, Lally, and Weir had done it—they had reached their high point, especially Ant. They had killed someone and gotten away with it. What more was there?

"My personal theory," Jim pondered, "is that [Ant] felt that he's had his high, high up: They had just killed somebody and got away with it." Part of that "high" involved Ant taking Marina's knickknacks and placing them in the house next to the walls, lined up like target apples or cans. Then they'd throw knives or shoot at them with crossbows. At the time, Jim viewed it as another way for

Ant to grieve. "It wasn't my place to judge how the guy mourned his aunt's passing."

But then they bought a grenade launcher and went out into the woods and started to launch grenades.

Grenades!

Scary, sure. Crazy, absolutely. But maybe just another way, Jim considered, of acting out and finding something to entertain what Jim viewed as a grieving kid with all this money to spend and happiness not for sale.

But there came a time during the summer of 2002 when Ant became quiet and everything changed. When the money didn't seem to stimulate him anymore, and the toys he bought became boring, Ant went in search of a new incentive to get up every morning.

"It was like this role playing game," Jim explained. "That none of us"—Lally and Weir, included—"were all that interested in."

At one point, Jim went over to Ant's apartment and, "I counted like twenty-five spiral-bound notebooks in where [Ant] was writing all these stories."

Those stories would soon turn into Ant's new reality. He'd take "thirty to forty people at a time," Jim said, and head out into the woods. "They'd all sit down together. They all had ranks." It was an imaginary *Lord of the Flies* world Ant had created all by himself. "It was like this weird cult type of thing . . . pretty messed up."

What Jim learned was that Ant had made up this "gothic, dark world, in which he was the leader . . . people would come to him and ask to be part of this world . . . part of another world."

Ant's version of Dungeons and Dragons.

Some of Ant's pawns would go into the woods, Jim said, early in the morning, and sit in the same place until midnight. All under Ant's orders.

"Ant had crazy manipulation powers."

But as the fall of 2002 came, Ant's money was almost gone. Corvette. Booze. Drugs. Parties. The ultimate reality game. He had pissed away hundreds of thousands of dollars on nothing.

"He bought insane amounts of mercenary equipment," Jim said. "He used have all these fatigues, they would tie each other up and say, 'Okay, you have a minute and a half to get out of it.' And they'd, like, rip their skin off just to get out of it."

With little money left, Ant started thinking about selling Marina's house. He needed some cash. He was out of his mind.

At the same time, Jason Weir wanted to exit the group. According to Jim, Weir was looking to get his life back on track. Weir sat with Jim in a TGIF restaurant on October 13, 2002, eating, thinking, talking, when the subject came up. To Jim, the dinner was like old times. The two of them just sitting, BS-ing about life. The chaos of Ant and his wild life was outside the door, an arm's length away. But inside that restaurant, two friends were discussing their futures—and none of that crazy behavior of Ant's mattered for that moment. They had the band. They talked about how good things were going. A recording deal, perhaps. Tour. The women. The fun.

But there was Ant. Always there. They both commented on how crazy all their lives had gotten since Marina's death. It had been almost ten months by then. Ant was out of control. He had lost his mind.

"My little sister," Jason Weir told Jim, "I need to be a good role model for her."

Jim nodded his head in agreement. It was heartbreaking for him to hear such a thing. He knew how deep in the group had gotten themselves. Here was Jason Weir wanting to get out of it all and lead a somewhat normal life and he felt that he couldn't.

When they began talking in more depth about Ant, Jim could tell Weir was harboring a secret that weighed heavily on him. Ant,

Jim soon learned from Weir, had a good reason for the role-playing Dungeons and Dragons/*Lord of the Flies* club he had started.

"He wanted to escape reality," Jim said. "I knew this once Jay [Weir] started telling me about what happened to Marina."

"He spent all his money," Weir said.

"Damn," Jim responded. "We need to get you on track, though, Jay."

Weir had an odd look about him. "Marina," he said quietly, leaning in toward Jim, looking around the restaurant to see if anyone was watching or listening, "she didn't exactly die on her own."

"What? What do you mean?" Jim was floored by the comment. At first, he thought, *I don't want to know anything more . . . don't tell me anything . . . I don't want to know.*

"Tom [Lally]," Weir whispered, "he beat her to death."

"Huh?" The thoughts running through Jim's mind were of his own grandmother, a fragile woman, like Marina, being beaten by three kids. What Marina must have gone through. The pain. The fear. The unreal fact of her grandson's friends beating her to death. Her last moments.

"What happened?" Jim asked.

"Tom hit her with a frying pan."

"What were you doing?" Jim wanted to know.

"I was just freaked out."

Jim was in a rough spot when he left TGIF in Norton with Jason Weir on October 13, 2002, after they talked some more about what had happened.

What should I do? Turn in my friends?

If Jim didn't tell someone, he was now part of it.

When Jim got home, he went straight to his father.

"My dad said that by me going to him and asking him what to do, I knew inside that he was going to go to the police if I didn't."

"I was thinking I was going to do this all anonymously, no one would ever know anything about me—walk in, walk out."

Mr. Good Samaritan.

Uh . . . not quite.

At home, preparing to go to the police in Norton, Jim began to think about his friend, Anthony Calabro. Jim had always viewed Ant as a sort of lost soul, a kid who never really fit in with any specific group. That alternate reality Ant had created out in the woods, Jim realized, was because his own life was such a complete waste. Ant needed a place, Jim mused, where "he was a God and he had all these minions . . . and none of these horrible things had happened. That he wasn't just some random guy."

Jim felt sorry for him.

Still, the thing to do was go to the police.

Knocking on the glass partition separating him from the Norton cop who was sitting, reading a magazine on that late Sunday night when Jim and his dad walked into the stationhouse, Jim said, "I guess I want to . . . well, like, I don't know, report a murder."

Jim thought bells and whistles would go off after he said it. That the cops would drop everything and roll out the red carpet for him. Come on in. Tell us what happened. You're a hero, son.

But that's not how it went.

The cop looked up from his magazine, handed Jim a slip of paper, and said, "Fill that out. Someone will be out to speak with you in a minute."

So Jim sat and wrote down exactly what he had discussed with Jason Weir earlier that day inside the TGIF.

At the time Jim walked into the police station, he was well known—not in a good way, mind you—by the same cops he was now going to ask to be his allies.

After a while, Jim was led into an interview suite in the back of the police station.

Two detectives soon came into the room.

Jim was making some fairly strong allegations here. Who's to say he wasn't coming in to cover his own ass?

"What is it about Sundays," Jim said one of the cops said aloud, mockingly, "that everyone likes to confess on Sundays."

Jim looked at the cop. "What? I didn't do this!" To himself, Jim thought, *What if I actually get blamed for this?* One better: What if, when confronted with Jim's story, Weir, Lally, and Ant pointed a finger at Jim and said he was there, too?

"They [the detectives] rode me and wouldn't let me leave the police station," Jim said. "For hours."

After answering the same questions repeatedly, Jim felt the interview wasn't going anywhere. He believed he was being backed into a corner by the detectives. And they didn't want to let him leave.

"I can prove myself," Jim blurted out.

"How?" one of the detectives asked.

"I'll wear a wire. I'll record Jay saying that he did it."

Four days went by before Jim could call his friend and set up a meeting. The police needed a court order to wire Jim.

And then, with a phone call, Jim was told it was time.

So he went down to the stationhouse, got wired up, and then he returned home and called Jason Weir.

"Jay, can you pick me up? I need to go to the mall to get a sweater."

"Sure. Be right over," Weir said.

Jim was ready. He had several undercover cops ready to follow him and Weir wherever they went. The game was on.

Scared doesn't even begin to describe how Jim felt. One of the main reasons, he explained, turned out to be that, "One, I know that Jay always carries a gun with him, or at least a knife. He's very, very protective."

The day before the meeting, Jim's dad suggested he carry his grandfather's gun.

Two guns, Jim knew, equaled a showdown.

He wanted no part of the OK Corral.

As Weir was on his way over, Jim sat and thought about the day: *Just get him to admit it again and get back home. Get it over with and get out of there.*

"But after he picked me up," Jim later recalled. "That's when things got really, really crazy."

—⁓—

Jason Weir picked Jim up on schedule. Weir was calm. He seemed okay. As they drove away, Jim said, "You know what, before we go out to the mall, can we stop to get a burger or something? I'm starving."

"Sure." (Jim was thinking, *I'm going to get this done and over with right now. First three minutes into our lunch.*)

They sat down.

"Hey, that stuff you told me a few days ago," Jim said, "was pretty disturbing."

Weir thought for a moment. "Oh yeah, you mean about the murder."

"Yeah, yeah."

"Oh . . ." Weir said—and, all over again, he proceeded to explain to Jim what happened.

They finished eating. *That was easy enough.* Jim could go get his sweater, go home, and be done with it all.

But then the unexpected happened (doesn't it always!). Weir was driving toward the mall. Jim was sitting shotgun thinking he had the entire thing in the bag. Then something went wrong.

"We're being followed," Weir said, looking in the rearview mirror. "Do you know we're being followed, Jim?"

"What? Shit. No way," Jim said, looking in the mirror. (To himself: *Those stupid cops. Damn it all.*)

"These cops couldn't even stay back far enough so Jay couldn't see them," Jim recalled. "I warned them that they all watch

Forensic Files and *CSI* and all those shows. They study this stuff. Stupid cops."

Then the car following behind—because the cops could hear what was being said inside Weir's truck—fell back and disappeared.

The situation got worse, however.

Jason Weir's cell phone rang. "Yeah?" he said. ("This phone call," Jim explained, "haunts my dreams to this day!") Weir started screaming into the phone. "What the fuck! The cops are at my house right now? They think I did *what?*"

What was Weir talking about?

Someone had called to warn Weir that there were cops at his house looking for him.

Jim couldn't believe it. The cops were jumping in now?

As Weir continued talking, Jim thought: *I should have grabbed that gun my dad wanted me to.*

Weir sped up. He was cruising now at about 65 to 70 miles per hour.

I should bail out. Right now. Jump out of this truck . . .

Weir hung up as he drove.

Jim was worried that Weir, if he knew Jim was wearing a wire, would "kill me and kill himself right there."

After Weir hung up, he looked at Jim with the "most disgusted look" he could muster.

Jim asked, "What happened, man?"

"I don't even want to talk about it."

From there, Weir pulled off the highway and sped toward what Jim called a "really shady-looking apartment building."

He parked. Looked at Jim. All business now, Weir said, "Get out. Come with me."

Jim was sweating. He wondered if he should make a run for it or go in. He looked around and didn't see any of his cop friends. Weir had lost the tail.

Shit.

Jim risked it, he said, and went inside with Weir. There were five or six guys in the apartment, Jim recalled, "and they're all, like, tripping and messed up."

"Jim, just go into that bedroom over there," Weir said, pointing, "and wait for me."

Jim walked in and began looking around for anything he could use as a weapon. There were no windows. So he sat on the bed.

Weir entered a few minutes later. He sat down. Flipped his cell phone open and dialed a friend.

Come to find out, Jim was worrying about nothing. Apparently, several cops had gone to Weir's house to question him about another matter entirely—a burglary. It had nothing to do with Marina's death.

"Jim," Weir said, "you gotta help me out, man. I was never there. You gotta tell the cops I was with you. They think I broke into this house."

"Sure, man, whatever you need." Jim was shaking. He couldn't control his body. "Let's just go get my sweater, Jay. Let's get out of here."

Jim told his friend, as they settled back into Weir's truck and got back on the road, "One last time . . . I want you to tell me what happened one last time and I never want to talk about it ever again. If there's ever a problem, I want to know the entire story so I can help you."

Jim's nerves were so frayed, he said later, that when Weir told the story again, adding more "sick details" than he had before, it nearly put Jim over the edge.

After Weir finished and Jim collected himself, he said, "Okay, there's murder weapons hidden in the woods. Let's go find them *right* now."

Weir drove out into the woods where he thought the weapons had been hidden, but they couldn't find anything. It was getting dark.

The next day, Jim took detectives out to the same spot and they found some newspapers from the date Marina had been killed, in which they believed the weapons had been wrapped. But the weapons were not there.

Nevertheless, law enforcement had enough to make three arrests; but they couldn't do it right away, Jim was told.

"What?" He wanted it over. He wanted Jason Weir, Thomas Lally, and Anthony Calabro taken into custody immediately. He had just ratted out his three best friends. He needed this over.

The Massachusetts State Police put together a case against Thomas Lally first. By October 25, 2002, several detectives headed over to Lally's Taunton Avenue home in Norton to pick Lally up and charge him with Marina Calabro's murder.

Lally gave himself up without as much as a snort.

Sergeant Kevin Shea, from the MSP, and Lieutenant Paul Keenan, from the QPD, brought Lally into an interview room inside the Norton Police Department.

Shea went through procedure and had Lally agree and sign all of his Miranda rights into effect.

"We have information," Shea began, "that leads us to believe you were involved with Anthony Calabro and Jason Weir in conspiring and killing . . . Marina Calabro."

Thomas Lally stared.

"Can you tell us how the plot to murder Ms. Calabro began?" Shea asked.

Lally went quiet for a brief moment. Then shrugged. "Sure. It started with Anthony."

"How do you know Anthony?" Shea asked.

"I met him through an old girlfriend. We hung out together. Anthony never had any money. He liked to play that game

Dungeons and Dragons. . . . Anthony always thought he was a tough guy. He acted like it. He wanted to be a hit man. . . . Anthony was always being bullied, so, you know, I never thought anything about what he said . . . but he kept persisting to be this tough guy."

The story Lally told seemed to make sense with how a murder plot like this—so vicious, callous, and ruthless, a senseless act of violence built around a staple of greed and selfishness—could have taken place over the course of a year. According to Lally, Ant started visiting Marina in Quincy more and more as she handed money over and wrote checks for anything Ant wanted. This seemingly endless flow of cash whetted Ant's appetite, however, and made him want more. And then one day, Lally said, "Anthony told me he would inherit a lot of money when she died."

And the seed was planted.

When Ant entered his "hit man" stage, when all he ever talked about was starting his own business and killing people for money, the subject came up, Lally said: "Anthony would joke around, saying, 'I should take out a contract on her [Marina].'" So there was one day when Lally called him on it—"What if, Ant, something just *happened* to her?"

Months went by. Ant and Lally would discuss killing Marina at various times, Lally said. Then, as they were sitting around getting high and Marina was out shopping one afternoon, Lally said Anthony brought it up again: "Well, this needs to be done."

Lally then described the murder in detail.

It was near 3:30 p.m. Thomas Lally approached Marina with a frying pan he had placed inside a pillowcase. Ant had left the apartment after learning what Lally was about to do. Ant's job was to act as a lookout outside, to make sure no one disrupted the murder.

"What are you doing with that frying pan?" Marina asked Lally.

"I'm doing this!" Lally said, smashing Marina in the head.

She screamed. So Lally grabbed Marina by the head and wrestled with her inside the kitchen.

She fell near the stove.

With Marina on the ground, Lally grabbed a teapot and bashed her in the head several times. Then he choked her, screaming into her ear, "Just go . . . just go . . . Anthony wants it this way."

"Anthony, help me . . . help me . . ." Marina had said loud as she could.

Within a few moments of being choked, Marina passed out.

Lally put a pillowcase over her head and suffocated the woman to make certain she was dead.

With Marina lying cold on the floor, Lally heard Ant in the hallway outside the door talking to someone. (It was Menz, who had come by while Ant was in the truck sitting with his dog outside.)

When he was done talking to Menz, Ant opened the door, saw Marina, nodded his head, and went back outside to his truck.

Lally realized Marina had caught him on the face with her nails and bit him. He had deep gouges and bite marks. Knowing what he knew from watching all those forensic shows, Lally cleaned underneath all of Marina's fingernails, scraping off any DNA.

Then he and Lally cleaned the apartment spotlessly.

In planning the murder, Lally had placed newspapers over the floor. After collecting the newspapers into a pile, he placed the teapot, frying pan, pot holders he had used, and anything else with blood on it (from the gash in Marina's head), into a plastic bag and put the bag in the back of his truck.

The deed was done.

～✦～

Later that night, October 25, 2002, Jason Weir and Anthony Calabro were arrested. In March 2006, Thomas Lally was convicted of first-degree murder in the slaying of Marina Calabro after a short trial and is now serving a life sentence without the possibility of parole. That June, Ant pleaded guilty to second-degree murder for acting as a lookout. He will be eligible for parole after serving fifteen years.

"I know that no words that I say will ever bring back Marina," Ant said in an apology to his family members present in court for his sentencing. "I'm disgusted with myself. I'm disgusted with my lack of action in attempting to stop it or anything else for that matter."

In exchange for his testimony against Lally, Jason Weir, who had helped plan the crime, agreed to plead guilty to manslaughter. He received a ten-year sentence.

But then there was Jim Morel—the guy who had turned in his friends. If you recall, my true-crime tale began with Jim being attacked and slashed with a knife as he jogged.

Whatever came of that? you might be asking at this point.

Jim made it home that day after being stabbed by two men who had obviously wanted him dead. Jim's mother walked into the bathroom while he was cleaning himself up.

"Oh my God, Jimmy, what happened?"

"I was attacked . . ."

Mrs. Morel called the police.

When the police showed up, one of the officers asked Jim what happened. According to Jim, he explained that he had been attacked by two knife-wielding men driving a blue car. They had to be part of Ant's group. This was payback. Jim had broken one of the golden rules of the street: He had given up his boys.

The cop said, "Oh no, no . . . we were in that area, we would have seen or heard something."

"I was attacked, man. Can't you see that I'm bleeding?" Jim said.

Jim Morel admitted that he had always had a "kind of touch and go relationship with the police." He was a punk during his youth. But this—to accuse him of slicing up his own skin, as he had felt the cops were suggesting, how could they even think such a thing?

Those two guys who slashed up Jim's arm were never caught.

The cops told Jim to file a complaint if he wanted to.

Jim never did.

CHAPTER 7

No Signs of Life

January 2006: Lanesborough, Massachusetts

TO BEGIN WITH, THERE IS NO DOUBT THAT FORTY-TWO-YEAR-OLD Patricia Olsen made a phone call to Mrs. O's, the seafood restaurant she owned, first thing in the morning on January 10, 2005, a typically frigid winter day in New England. We know this because, according to the court testimony of Mrs. O's employee Rosa Nicola, Patricia phoned in the same request she had on most other mornings. We are, after all, creatures of habit, if nothing else.

"Rosa," Patricia said in her scratchy, smoker's voice, "can you bring me a breakfast sandwich over to the house for Neil." Neil Olsen, a big man with brown hair and a resolute smile, a country boy at heart, was Patricia's forty-eight-year-old husband of twelve years.

Everybody liked Neil Olsen.

"Certainly, Mrs. Olsen," Rosa answered.

Mrs. O's was located just down the road from Neil and Patricia Olsen's home on South Main Street, just outside downtown Lanesborough, Massachusetts. It took Rosa only a few minutes to make the sandwich and get it over to the house.

Patricia greeted Rosa at the door and, as usual, invited her in, feeling the need to say (for some strange reason), "I didn't sleep well last night. I took three Tylenol PM pills."

Idle chit-chat between an employer and her employee, or so it seemed. Patricia adored Rosa. Most people did. Rosa was a hard worker, one of only a few Patricia had hired in the two years since she'd opened the restaurant.

Rosa nodded. "Okay, Mrs. Olsen."

Patricia later told police, "Neil eats breakfast every morning. I don't normally eat breakfast, maybe once a week." Rosa was good about bringing Neil his breakfast every morning. It was her routine. Later, in court, Patricia recalled a time when Rosa went on vacation. "I thought Neil was going to go nuts. I hate cooking breakfast."

Upon entering the Olsen household, Rosa wondered where Neil was.

"He's out in the barn," Patricia explained. "I think he's working."

Rosa put the sandwich down on the counter and drove back to the restaurant. It would be the last ordinary, routine situation Rosa and Patricia ever experienced together. Moments after Rosa left, around 8:00 a.m., Lanesborough Police Chief F. Mark Bashara arrived for work and a 911 call came into the Lanesborough Police Department (LPD), a call that rocked this quaint New England town off its axis.

❧

The 911 caller was Patricia Olsen. She was frantic. Terribly upset. She said she'd just found Neil dead in the barn, a separate building connected to his sign-making workshop, not too far away from the house where he and Patricia lived. She had no idea what happened. She had gone out to bring him his morning coffee and breakfast sandwich when she saw the most horrible thing.

Bashara had known Neil and Patricia for several years. Neil was a local business owner, a sign maker. For the most part, Neil lettered trucks and cars. He was quite the whiz with a brush and some paint and had an excellent reputation in town. Not a soul in Lanesborough had anything bad to say about old Neil Olsen's work, not to mention his character.

Bashara soon heard that Neil had been found dead in his barn, and that Patricia was beside herself. She couldn't tell what happened. Soon after realizing something was terribly wrong (. . . *my goodness, all that blood, Neil just lying there, still as a sack of potatoes* . . .), Patricia explained to Bashara, she ran back into the kitchen to call 911.

"I thought he had fallen," Patricia said later. "I thought he had a heart attack."

Bashara and a colleague hopped in two separate cruisers and raced out to the Olsen place. Between the time Patricia called 911 and Bashara arrived, Patricia called Rosa Nicola again and explained how she had found Neil in the barn. She told Rosa she believed Neil was dead.

Startled and quite upset by this, Rosa rushed over to the house.

When she got there, Rosa later recalled, Patricia was "standing over the kitchen sink, vomiting."

When Patricia finished, she and Rosa sat down. Rosa knew Neil well. She liked him. It was indescribable to think he was dead. Impossible to believe. How could it have happened? Neil was one of those guys always there. Always working around the house, driving through town in his truck, waving to friends and neighbors. He never went far from town.

"That horse killed him!" Patricia blurted out to Rosa's surprise. Patricia was speaking of Neil's beloved horse, Hannah. Every night, like clockwork, Neil went out to the barn between 11:00 and 11:30 p.m. to feed Hannah. Apparently, Patricia had slept through the night after taking those three Tylenol PMs, unaware that Neil hadn't returned to bed from the routine feeding.

"What?" Rosa asked. She had a hard time swallowing the notion that Neil's own horse had killed him.

"It's my fault," Patricia said. Now the widow was crying. She was almost hysterical. Blaming herself. "I took too many pills. Otherwise I would have been awake."

~ ~

Located in the eastern region of Massachusetts, quite close to the border of New York, Lanesborough is part of Berkshire County. The Pittsfield (Massachusetts) metro area is due south. With just under three thousand residents, Lanesborough's median household income comes in at about $46,000, which is $5,000 more than the national average. Lanesborough is not considered a mecca for crime. Not at all. In fact, the last murder here occurred in 1980, some twenty-three years before Neil Olsen's questionable death. Lanesborough residents, we could say without argument, are used to going about their business and never having the thought of being accosted or bothered with the kind of crime that has beleaguered other Berkshire towns. Murder rates—that is, rates for violent crime of any sort—were so low here between the years 1980 and 2000 that there were only nine rapes and four robberies throughout that entire span of time, on top of the one murder in 1983. With numbers like those, it's safe to say that Lanesborough is one of the safest places on the planet to live.

Still, when the alarm bells rang at the LPD announcing an untimely death had occurred out at the Olsen place, it wasn't that the LPD were unprepared, it's just that murder would have been the last thing on any cop's mind as he or she pulled up and began to look at the scene. Murder just didn't happen in these parts.

Patricia was convinced that Neil had been trampled to death by Hannah, his beloved thirty-one-year-old former trotter race horse; at least that was her early impression when LPD chief Mark Bashara arrived on that chilly morning moments after Patricia's 911 call.

"We believed at the time," Bashara said later, describing the crime scene, "that Neil Olsen was actually killed by the horse."

Inside the barn where Neil kept Hannah, Bashara walked into a bloody mess the likes of which he had probably never seen in his decades behind the badge. The horse, undoubtedly spooked, was making snorting sounds and running wild around the inside of the barn. And Hannah had blood all over her.

Patricia was "distraught," Bashara added. She was sitting at the kitchen table inside the house when he first arrived: smoking, speaking in broken sentences, crying, shaking her head. Patricia couldn't believe what had happened. Of all things, Neil, who had so much adored his beautiful Hannah, had been trampled to death by the same animal he loved so dearly! How could an animal turn on its owner like this—especially a horse?

To Patricia, however, as she sat and thought about it more and more, Hannah's killing Neil, well, it didn't seem all that surprising to her after all. "Hannah is a thirty-one-year-old miserable bitch," was how Patricia described the horse to police. "We've had her for, I think, three years. We got her from some friend of Neil's. . . . I say Hannah is miserable because she doesn't let anyone ride her. Neil bought me a saddle a couple of years ago. I wanted a horse to ride. At night, he always let the horse in because she won't listen to me. . . . The routine is to bring her in and give her a can of grain." Patricia had put the horse in the barn only "once," she said. "Even if Neil fell asleep before eleven, he would get up and bring Hannah in at around eleven thirty."

After speaking with Patricia, Bashara entered Neil's sign shop, just beyond the breezeway almost connecting the house to the barn, and he re-entered the barn. As he approached Neil's body, he could see there wasn't much left to Neil's head. The scene was horrific. The veteran chief looked down and noticed Neil's face was nearly gone, his head nothing but an unrecognizable slush of blood, tissue, and brain. Neil's face and head had been smashed to bits, as if someone had taken a sledgehammer to a melon. Perhaps equally disturbing to Bashara as he stood looking at Neil was that he had once hired Neil to letter some of the police cruisers. Bashara knew and liked Neil Olsen.

After Bashara had a look at Neil's remains, he called in one of his coworkers, Officer Jim Rathbun, and radioed the Massachusetts State Police Detective Unit. Before he released this scene and wrote the whole thing off as a terrible accident, it was worth having the big boys come in and take a quick look, see what they thought.

Officer Jim Rathbun was down the road when he took Bashara's call. Arriving at the Olsen house by approximately 8:45 a.m., Rathbun and Bashara "secured" what they were now calling a bona fide crime scene. Just to be certain. Whether a horse had committed the act or not, Neil Olsen was dead, that much was a fact, and the barn was potentially the scene of a homicide. Detectives would have to investigate. The integrity of the scene needed to be protected.

There was a solid, well-packed coating of snow on the ground around the Olsen property and all about town. It was overcast, thirty-two degrees Fahrenheit. The wind blew in from the southwest at about ten miles per hour. A recent snowstorm had pummeled the region, burying Lanesborough and the surrounding communities. But on this morning, Bashara, if he had wanted to, could have looked out on eight miles of visibility, despite the ripening conditions for another major Nor'easter.

Rathbun closed the gate inside the barn to seal off Neil's body from Hannah; this way, the horse couldn't taint the crime scene any more than she had already.

As Rathbun shut the gate, the horse got nervous and restless, and Rathbun had to hurriedly go about his business, "afraid," he later said, "of the horse."

After that, Rathbun walked into the kitchen of the main house, where Patricia was sitting at the kitchen table, still shaken up and crying, chain-smoking cigarettes. ("She appeared very upset, very distraught," Rathbun recalled.)

"I cannot believe this is happening," Patricia lashed out to no one in particular. Her husband, her confidant, as she later put it, the one man she had loved more than any other, was gone. Just like that. Puff! Here one minute, dead the next.

What the hell happened?

"Please, somebody wake me up!" Patricia said.

Rathbun asked Patricia what she and Neil had done the previous night. He was making idle chit-chat, perhaps, waiting for MSP detectives to arrive and assess the situation. The woman obviously needed someone to sit with and talk—or, rather, listen.

Patricia suffered from Crohn's disease, same as three of her four sisters. Crohn's is a debilitating intestinal tract disorder that can knock a person down and keep him or her bedridden for days, in some cases weeks. Some even die from long-term complications.

"Three [of Patricia's sisters] ended up with Crohn's disease," a family member later told me. "One of Pat's sisters died in 2000 of complications from cancer so widespread, when they found it, there was nothing doctors could do. She had just turned forty-three the week she died."

"I took some Tylenol," Patricia told Rathbun. "I went to bed after playing video games with Neil."

("She often took the Tylenol," a family member later explained to me, "routinely, because of her Crohn's disease.")

"What about this morning?" Rathbun asked.

"I woke up and found the television still on. I assumed Neil was already in the shop working."

Neil was a workaholic. Having his shop connected to his home further contributed to his obsessive work ethic.

Rathbun said later that he asked Patricia about Hannah—and that's when she became annoyed and angry, lashing out, saying, "The horse would sometimes kick us" if poked in a way that wasn't to its liking. Temperamental, that damn horse. Spoiled rotten. "I want that horse gone," Patricia raged to Rathbun, "or I'll kill it myself."

It seemed Patricia couldn't bear to look at the horse again, knowing what it had done to her husband.

At this point Patricia started ranting about "funeral costs" and not having enough insurance to cover Neil's subsequent burial. The man hadn't even been lifted from the scene of his death and his wife was worried about spending money she claimed she didn't have.

To say the least, this little ripple in Patricia's story sent up red flags.

After Rathbun finished talking with Patricia, he met with Bashara outside. By then, detectives from the MSP had arrived. State Trooper Jean Thibodeau approached the two local cops and asked about what they had found earlier upon arrival. Then Thibodeau went into the barn with the medical examiner, who himself had just pulled up to the scene, and began processing the barn, hunting for more information—answers to this bizarre set of circumstances.

Walking across horse manure and hay, Thibodeau bent down and took a closer look at Neil's head, asking herself, *Could a horse have done this? Was it even possible?*

After assessing the scene, Thibodeau searched around the floor of the barn near Neil's head. She spied several small-caliber, spent shell casings.

It was odd, or maybe just a coincidence, that there were shell casings in the barn. Perhaps Neil had taken target practice from inside the barn? Maybe he pressed his own ammunition?

Was the guy a hunter?

Thibodeau walked out of the barn and combed the immediate area for more evidence that might explain what had happened. There had to be something else. Something they were missing.

Within a few moments, the detective turned a corner in back of the barn and, just beyond the barn doors, there in the snow, she spotted something that was about to turn this investigation on its head.

—◆—

Patricia Olsen grew up in Bennington, Vermont. A family member said she was no different than any other kid. Being the youngest of all girls, Patricia was of course playing catch up all the time. When one of her sisters graduated early from high school under an accelerated program, Patricia wanted to do the same thing. So, at fifteen years old, she went to her mother and asked.

Patricia's mother, however, said the only way she'd "approve it" was if Patricia agreed to go to college after graduation.

"Yes," Patricia told her mother. "I'll do that."

But as soon as she graduated, Patricia put college off for a year. During that time, she met James Robinson, a local kid.

"James was the only boyfriend Patricia ever had," that family member told me.

Foregoing college, Patricia chose to marry James a year later, soon after she turned eighteen. But it didn't last long. In 1989, after having two kids, Christopher and Amanda Robinson, Patricia divorced James. A year after the divorce, Patricia started commuting to Pittsfield, working as a comptroller for Lenco, an armored truck company. Getting away from the town she grew up in, if only to work, was important to Patricia. Although Bennington was home to some fifteen thousand people, Pittsfield was much larger at forty-five thousand. The two towns were only twenty-five miles away from each other, but worlds apart. Pittsfield offered Patricia a fresh start. Different people. A new scene. Since high school, she had dated one man, become a housewife and mother, and never really had a chance to have a life beyond small-town Bennington. Now she was single for what was effectively the first time, fully prepared to take on life. The kids, Amanda and Christopher, ended up staying with their father in Bennington. Patricia didn't abandon them, she and a family member later said, but since she suffered so badly from Crohn's, she felt she couldn't work and handle the children at the same time.

By then, Neil had been in the sign-making business for about five years. He did a lot of business with Lenco. One day, while at the office, Neil bumped into Patricia and, after she "openly flirted" with him, they started talking.

"I used to pay him," Patricia told police, "when he got done lettering."

Neil did the work; Patricia cut him a check.

Unbeknownst to her, Neil was in love.

Then, in March 1993, Neil got up the nerve to approach Patricia with an offer. "I need to talk to you," he said one afternoon after she handed him his check.

"Oh," Patricia remarked. "About what?"

Neil didn't say. Instead, he invited her to his house in Lanesborough that night.

Intrigued and admittedly having a "crush" on Neil, Patricia agreed to dinner.

"I fell in love with you the first time I saw you," Neil told Patricia that night.

She was stunned.

But there was more.

"You know," Neil continued, "we're always busy while at work." He said he'd never had the opportunity to express how he felt. Yet things were different now. He felt the need to speak out. Patricia was all he thought about. "This may sound strange," Neil said at some point after dinner, "but I want you to move in with me."

Patricia was speechless.

Neil walked over to a desk in his living room. "I have something for you," he said, opening the drawer. In Patricia's words, the rest of the night went like this: "He said he was going to give me a 'get out of this relationship free card,' so if I did move in with him and things didn't work out, I could just leave. He opened his desk drawer and he gave me this stupid plastic skull ring because he said it was all he had for rings."

An otherwise shy and ascetic guy, Neil popped the question, handing Patricia the toy ring. When Patricia left Neil's house, she called a friend and explained what happened. "You're insane," her friend said after Patricia admitted she was thinking about moving in. "You don't even *know* this guy."

Patricia never "even thought about it," she claimed. She moved in the following Monday.

On May 28, 1994, in a field behind Neil's house, Neil waited beside sixty guests, mostly family and friends, as Patricia drove up the hill to the altar in her Bronco, bridesmaids by her side, cheering her on. A redneck wedding if there ever was one!

After a lovely ceremony amid a perfect New England setting on a beautiful spring afternoon, Neil and Patricia were husband and wife. According to Patricia, for years things between them went well. They loved, laughed, and enjoyed a healthy, uncomplicated relationship.

"It was all fun," she later said, describing those early years.

Neil had graduated from Pittsfield High School in 1974. After that, he studied at Southeastern Massachusetts University, later completing a degree in business administration at Berkshire Community College. Going into business for himself seemed to fit Neil's nature, friends and family said. After taking a job at several local sign companies—Pittsfield Neon Sign, Industrial Sign, and Callahan Sign Company among them—and working toward his full apprenticeship, Neil decided to open up a shop of his own. Almost immediately, Neil's reputation as a master sign-maker worked its way around Berkshire County. He was known not for painting simple signs, but works of art on fire engines, cars, and trucks, along with designing and painting signs for local and national businesses of all types. Neil loved the isolation of retreating to his sign shop and losing himself in his work. There was no mistaking a sign Neil Olsen had made. The craftsmanship alone marked his unique professional signature.

Beyond a love for sign-making, Neil, a member of the United Methodist Church in Lenox, Massachusetts, took great comfort in rebuilding, detailing, and refinishing antique cars and trucks—hobbies that fell under the same umbrella as his professional life. It was the meticulous nature of taking something old and making it new again that Neil adored. Yet it was animals that Neil treasured most. His horse Hannah, of course. But also his two dogs, Cletis, a two-year-old bloodhound, and Bosco, a four-year-old mixed Labrador. Both dogs slept upstairs with Neil and Patricia. Cletis was so big, in fact, Patricia and Neil placed a full-size mattress on the floor next to their bed so he was comfortable at night. It was Bosco who had initially found Neil dead. The dog, obviously confused about what had happened, lay down next to Neil in the barn and waited until, Patricia claimed, she walked in with his morning breakfast sandwich and uncovered the ghastly scene. One of the things Neil gave his dogs, family and friends later explained to a local newspaper, was their freedom, essentially. He allowed the dogs to roam the wooded acres around his home. The dogs loved being able to come and go as they pleased.

Neil was a simple man, Patricia insisted, adding that he was never abusive. By June 1998, Patricia had custody of Amanda and

Christopher. They were fourteen and sixteen then. Neil thought it a good husbandly gesture to help Patricia, so they hired an attorney, sued James Robinson for custody, and won. As the kids fell into their new lives in Lanesborough, they started acting out as they both entered high school. Their grades plummeted during their high school years. They became arrogant, wise-ass, rebellious. Patricia tried her best to control them, but they rarely listened. Christopher, especially, was getting involved in some rather disturbing behavior. While he might have seemed to be a misguided youth, disobedient and undirected, Christopher's actions spoke of a dark and menacing seed he harbored, giving the indication that he was mentally unstable. For example, Amanda later said her brother once took a mouse, put it in a jar, filled the jar with lighter fluid, and lit it on fire. More than that, Christopher would go weeks without bathing. He wore all black, painted his hair different colors, and cut himself. He and a friend from school once made a list, Amanda said, that they referred to as a "death list." It consisted of teachers and other kids from school they wanted dead. Christopher downloaded directions from the Internet on how to make a bomb. He called himself an "Anarchist."

"That's when he got in big trouble. . . . He got suspended," Amanda later told police. "That's when Neil pulled him by his hair. Neil yelled at him. I don't remember Neil hitting him."

Amanda had her own problems. In eighth grade she was charged with assault after spiking a fellow classmate's drink with Tylenol. The kid was allergic to over-the-counter medicines and had a terrible reaction.

"My rules weren't working," Patricia said, talking about this period of Christopher and Amanda's lives. "So Neil decided he was going to take over disciplining them. I intervened once in a while," she added, "but . . . tried it and it wasn't working."

Neil took control, indeed. But had little patience. Whereas in most blended families the stress of raising someone else's kids can be detrimental to a marriage, Patricia claimed she and Neil hardly ever had problems because of it, and agreed for the most part on how to punish the kids when they acted out.

"He was my everything," Patricia said. The tension the kids caused in the house hadn't in any way, she insisted, "affected the marriage."

Christopher became more "distant" and eventually "withdrew" from everyone. He didn't want to be part of the family atmosphere at all. The further along he got into high school, the more despondent he became at home, which didn't sit well with Patricia.

But if the kids had changed since living in Lanesborough, so had Patricia.

"After she married Neil, the first two or three years, well, [she] had a very good relationship [with the family]," a family member later told me. "Then she just stopped associating with everyone, as if she was shut off from us. I don't know if it was by Neil or her. Up until today we have never known why. . . . It was so strange." There was no one event, in other words, triggering the disengagement. "One day she was just out of our lives. Which meant, as soon as Patricia and Neil got custody of the kids, [we] stopped seeing them, too."

Patricia later said Neil, in the beginning, wanted to teach the kids the strong work ethic he had displayed in front of them. He believed he could, by example, show the kids that hard work paid off. Part of his desire to take the time to teach the kids his ways was rooted, Patricia asserted, in his quest to "relieve" her of "the stress" she was experiencing trying to discipline them herself. But no sooner had Neil and Patricia put their foot down, than the kids' behavior got worse. During one period, Neil caught Amanda repeatedly smoking cigarettes in her room. So when simply telling her she wasn't allowed to smoke in the house didn't work, Neil grabbed his toolbox, unhinged her bedroom door, and hid it. Now there was an open portal into Amanda's private world. Part of

Neil's concern was that she was leaving ashes all over the place; he worried she'd burn the house down. Then Patricia and Neil found a bag of marijuana in Amanda's room. After rolling a bone and smoking it with Neil, Patricia later admitted, they discarded the remainder and punished the child.

Another time, when Amanda disobeyed a direct order, Neil brought her outside, put a large aluminum rake in her hands, and told her to "re-grade" the gravel driveway before digging a ditch near the edge of the yard.

This set a precedent with Amanda. She'd act out and get grounded. Then she was forced to do some sort of physical labor as punishment. But when that stopped working, Patricia and Neil grounded her (Amanda was sixteen) until she was eighteen.

Two full years.

"Every time we let her off, she would turn around and do something else," Patricia said. "She remained grounded throughout much of her high school years."

By this time Patricia had opened Mrs. O's. It had been a childhood dream to run her own restaurant. She was a great cook. A hard worker. And being out of the house much of the time didn't seem so bad lately, seeing that she was having so many problems with the kids.

As a comptroller, Patricia had supervised the financial affairs of Lenco. She was in control, basically, of how much money went out, how much was left. Now she was doing the same thing with Neil's sign-making business, her restaurant, and the household bills and expenses. Anything having to do with the finances, in effect, was under Patricia's governorship. Insurance. Mortgage. Car payments. Food.

All of it.

But if being able to control financial circumstances, at home and professionally, satisfied one aspect of Patricia's character, not being able to get a firm hold on the children consumed the other. Christopher wasn't doing any better. By the eleventh grade, Patricia and Neil were disappointed to learn Christopher had only accrued enough credits to be in ninth grade; he'd have to repeat two full grades and wouldn't graduate until two years after his class.

When the reality of the hard work ahead of him hit Christopher, he decided that going to school wasn't worth the effort any longer. He quit.

"Find yourself a job if you're not going to school," Neil told him, demanding that if Christopher was going to live in the house, he had damned well better have a job. "Either that, or get the hell out."

Meanwhile, by Amanda's own account later, she was getting actively involved in harder drugs. Then she and Christopher, after he moved out of the house, started hanging out together with the same crowd.

A runaway train was in motion—one Patricia later claimed she never saw heading off the tracks.

"One thing I've felt about [Christopher]," a blood relative told me, "was that beyond him being a pathological liar, being near him [later] actually gave me the chills."

❧

Back at the Olsen house on January 10, 2005, shortly after the MSP arrived, a discovery was made just beyond the barn doors that sent the investigation into a frenzy: "a bloody metal pipe." For an investigation at first centered on Hannah, the alleged murderous mare, cops were now looking at a dramatic turn of events.

As investigators continued working the scene, Patricia was still inside the house wandering around, reportedly distraught over her husband's untimely death.

While investigators were compiling evidence, talking over the situation, undoubtedly preparing to re-enter the house and question

Patricia more pointedly, Christopher Robinson, Patricia's son, called. Since being kicked out of the house by Neil, Christopher had lived at various locations—including in his car and wherever else he could find a place to crash. He had even spent some time with Amanda, who now lived with her boyfriend and his father in New York. Patricia, some of her employees later said, at times had even allowed Christopher to sleep at the restaurant, without telling Neil. But over the past few days, Christopher, with no job and certainly no money, had been living at a sleazy motel just up the road from the Olsen house.

"I want to come over and visit," Christopher said. Patricia understood that her son knew what had happened and was offering his support, to be there for her. But, at the same time, "He just didn't sound sympathetic," she later said.

So she told him no. He wasn't welcome.

Before Patricia had dialed 911 that morning, she said she "ran into the barn and touched Neil's leg and saw flashes of objects" around her, such as "Hannah's face and a coffee can filled with grain." What she didn't see—or so she claimed—was all the blood pooled around Neil's head—and there was plenty of it.

Now detectives had closed off the scene with yellow CSI tape. There was no doubt a homicide had occurred inside the barn. MSP Trooper Stephen Jones, out on the property with colleagues, spotted "a double set of footprints in snow," which led directly from Patricia's and Neil's house to the street. Then Jones, Trooper Carol Zullo, and a chemist, while searching the Skyline Country Club golf course just to the east of the Olsen property, came upon another set of footprints and traced them from the golf course to the Olsen house. While they were photographing the footprints, one of them spied a shiny item in the snow.

"What is it?" asked a trooper.

"Looks like a machete."

They bagged the weapon and went back to the house.

Patricia had called Casey Nicola, Rosa's daughter and also an employee of Mrs. O's, and asked her to come to the house. While Nicola was there consoling her boss, an officer stayed in the house with the two of them. At some point, the officer asked, "What about funeral arrangements?"

Patricia covered her ears, as if to say she didn't want to hear about anything related to Neil's death. It was all too much to take, she implied. "We have no insurance," Patricia finally answered. "I don't know what I'm going to do."

It was an odd statement. Although Mrs. O's wasn't doing all that well financially, it was still an active business, as was Neil's sign-making enterprise. Not to have insurance through either business—or both—seemed strange. The only way the insurance could have been dropped was if the Olsens had failed to keep up with the premiums.

Nicola went back to work. When she returned to the restaurant, she explained to Christopher, who had been hanging around there most of the morning, what had happened to Neil.

He said he had heard the news already.

"Go to your mother, Chris," Nicola suggested. "She needs you."

Christopher didn't seem to care. He shrugged it off, saying instead, "I'm going to the mall with a friend."

❦

On January 11, 2005, the Office of the State Medical Examiner in Holyoke, Massachusetts, released its findings regarding Neil Olsen's death. What a shocker. As the shell casings found near Neil's body had suggested, it was confirmed by the ME's office that Neil had been killed by gunshot wounds—a total of seven. More than that, the ME found out Neil had been beaten in the head with a blunt object, likely the metal pipe and/or the machete troopers had found outside the barn. The likely scenario seemed to be that Neil Olsen's murderer killed him with a shotgun, but then tried to cover it up by bludgeoning his head into a mess of tissue to make it appear as though he had been trampled to death by his horse.

With that information, detectives headed back over to the Olsen house to give Patricia the bad news: Someone had murdered her husband.

Detective Lieutenant Richard Smith, a twenty-seven-year veteran of the MSP, was first to tell Patricia they had changed the focus of their investigation. "We no longer believe Neil's horse killed him," Smith stated.

"I'm in shock," Patricia said. "I don't want to accept that Neil is gone."

Considering the circumstances, detectives had an entire new set of questions for the grieving widow. Number one, who might have wanted Neil dead? On the surface, the guy had no enemies. Why would someone kill him? The person responsible for Neil's death obviously hated Neil—that much was clear from the viciousness of the attack. It was no random murder. Nothing was missing from the barn or house. Neil's pockets had been turned inside out and his killer had taken any cash Neil had. But other than that, nothing appeared to be out of place. No tools were missing. No one had broken into the house. Patricia was even home, upstairs, according to her, sleeping off three Tylenol PMs, when seven shots interrupted an otherwise peaceful Berkshire night. She said she had not heard a peep.

Patricia's and Neil's bedroom was upstairs on the south side of their house, a family member later suggested, almost as far away from the barn as possible. It was late. There was no way she could have heard the shots, this source insisted. In fact, Patricia told detectives she fell asleep after playing a video game with Neil and having sex while *Desperate Housewives* and the beginning of *Boston Legal* played on television in the background. Neil must have gone out to the barn after Patricia had fallen asleep. On top of that, Patricia had a bad habit of falling asleep with the television on and claimed she needed to have the television on all night in order to sleep. In addition to the Tylenol, she'd had "three or four" glasses of white wine.

But cops wanted more. They asked Patricia if she was willing to head down to the LPD to give a statement.

She thought about it for a moment. "Sure."

At 12:35 p.m., after cops read Patricia her rights as a procedure, she talked about her last day with Neil. There was not an attorney present and Patricia freely offered all the information she could—with the hope, one would assume, of helping to find Neil's killer.

After talking about her life in Bennington and how she met Neil, Patricia went through the entire day. The detail she recalled was remarkable—as if she had written it all down and studied it. She said she "spent most of the day lying on the couch. I didn't feel well." After Neil ate French toast, he kept himself busy drywalling one of the bathrooms. Then one of her employees from the restaurant brought Neil's breakfast by the house after stopping at the local Getty gas station, under orders from Patricia, to pick her up a pack of cigarettes and the *National Enquirer* magazine.

Neil was a big fan of Spike Television programming. He loved the shows about cars and trucks. A man's man. Spike was running a marathon of car shows that day. By 10:30 a.m., Neil had taken a break from drywalling and settled down in the living room next to Patricia to watch a few of "his car shows."

At some point, Neil's parents, Ruth and Harold Olsen, stopped by. Patricia, who spent some time cleaning the house before they showed up, greeted the couple outside when they arrived.

"Ruthy," Patricia recalled to police, "went to hug me but I told her not to because I hadn't been feeling well."

"Where's Neil?" Ruth asked.

By then Neil had gone upstairs to play video games.

"I love his parents," Patricia recalled, "they have been good parents to me, but they never call before they come over. Neil and I get pissed off sometimes because we [like] our privacy."

Why would Patricia say she had cleaned the house if she hadn't known Ruth and Harold Olsen were stopping by? Both Christopher and Amanda later told police their mother had gotten extremely lazy the past few years and rarely cleaned anything. The house was filthy all the time. Rabbit and dog excrement were everywhere, Amanda claimed. And Patricia just left it there, besides allowing many of the pets to roam freely around the house and even sleep in her room on her bed. Cleaning was something Patricia had given up long ago.

Part of that privacy she and Neil enjoyed so much, Patricia said, included sex. Lots of it. Since Amanda had moved out, Patricia and Neil had the house all to themselves. "[We] had a *lot* of sex at different times of the day. When [Amanda] moved out last year, Neil said it was great because we could run around the house naked."

Ruth and Harold didn't stay long that Sunday. Patricia was in no mood to entertain. She wanted to do nothing more than rest, drink some wine, and spend time with her husband.

When Ruth and Harold left, Patricia made herself and Neil a "roast beef and cheese" sandwich. While Neil ate, he worked on a crossword puzzle. After they finished eating, Patricia sat down on the couch and turned on a movie. Neil went off and did a few chores, but ended up watching the end of the movie with her.

After the movie, Neil painted the dining room wall and put drywall compound on the walls in the bathroom. Near 3:30 p.m., he finished working and went upstairs to play video games again.

That's when Patricia phoned Amanda, who was living in New York with her boyfriend, who was in prison. Patricia wanted to know where the PlayStation games were. Neil was looking all over the house for a specific game and was really upset because he couldn't find it.

While they were on the phone, Amanda's boyfriend called from prison.

"I have to take the call, mother."

Patricia called back ten minutes later. They talked about several of Amanda's friends who were, according to Amanda, worried about getting AIDS. Drugs and unsafe sex between large groups of people is a good recipe for the spread of HIV. It was happening all around Amanda. She didn't know what to do. She was worried about a few of her girlfriends; each had slept with one or more of the guys who were thought to have been infected.

"We also talked about her work and how Amanda," Patricia said, "was demoted because she doesn't have a driver's license and how her hours were being cut back."

Both Amanda and Patricia described the conversation in similar ways. Patricia was worried about her daughter. She felt Amanda was running with a group of people no good for her. And with all the drugs floating around, Amanda might get caught up again. Ever since she'd had a problem with cocaine some time ago, which she had admitted to police and testified to in court, Amanda had been a good girl. But Patricia knew how tough peer pressure could be and worried about her.

Throughout the day, Patricia drank several glasses of wine. She liked wine in the box, she said. It helped her relax. At 7:15 p.m., she poured a fresh glass of boxed *vino* and went upstairs to spend time with Neil. He had found his PlayStation game by then.

"You want to race me?" Neil asked.

Patricia sat on the bed. "As long as we use separate controllers."

Neil often teased Patricia about having sweaty palms. He called her "Sweaty Betty" because of it.

"We played for a while . . . maybe fifteen minutes," Patricia said. "He kicked my ass."

Next, Patricia went downstairs to call Christopher's ex-girl-friend, the mother of her grandchild. Christopher and his girlfriend were estranged, but Patricia kept in touch with the girl. She worried about the baby. She and Neil would often slip $50 or $100 bills into the ex-girlfriend's diaper bag whenever she stopped by the house with the child, mainly because they knew Christopher never helped.

While they were talking, Patricia mentioned *Desperate House-wives* and said she had to get off the phone because she didn't want to miss the show. She and Neil loved to watch it together.

After Patricia and Neil watched *Housewives,* Neil got undressed and sat on the bed, saying with raised eyebrows, "I'm all ready."

"Neil sleeps in the nude and doesn't wear pajamas," Patricia commented.

With Neil in bed waiting for sex, Patricia went into the bathroom, undressed, and walked into the room naked.

"Neil was watching a law show [*Boston Legal*] with Captain Kirk in it, William Shatner," Patricia recalled. "We watched the show together."

At some point during the show, Patricia explained, they "made love—had intercourse. I couldn't really tell you what happened on the show."

As they started, Neil asked, "You okay?"

"Yeah," Patricia answered.

"Are you sure I'm not hurting you?"

"Yeah, I'm fine."

About fifteen minutes later, Patricia got up and went into the bathroom.

"I lied to Neil," she recalled. "It did kind of hurt. I was just really tired and wanted to have a good night's sleep."

After swallowing three Tylenol PMs, washing them down with a gulp of white wine, Patricia crawled into bed next to Neil and fell asleep—knowing, of course, that Neil was going out to the barn to feed Hannah at some point.

The remainder of Patricia's first statement to police details, primarily, the moments after she found Neil in the barn. Still, it wasn't the last time Patricia would sit with police and talk about the events leading up to her husband's murder. At the same time law enforcement interviewed Patricia, Troopers Brian Berkel and Michael Hill were up the road speaking to Christopher Robinson—which would send the investigation into a new direction entirely.

❧

About a half mile down the road from the Olsen house, the Mountain View Motel stood across the street from Pontoosuc Lake, a massive body of water bordering North Main Street (Route 7) on the eastern side. A rather tiny, cabin-like dwelling, with maybe six or seven rooms total, the motel houses travelers and visitors to the lake region, but mainly those who have nowhere to live and need a room by the night. Christopher had been expelled from the Olsen house by Patricia and Neil since the fall of 2004. In October of that year, Patricia wrote Christopher a "no trespass order," stating, "You are hereby notified to leave and remain away from the [restaurant] . . . as well as from the premises owned and occupied by Neil Olsen and his wife." Further, Patricia explained that she had "notified the public safety officials in . . . Pittsfield . . . and Lanesboro[ugh]. . . . If you appear at either of these premises in violation of this notice, you will be subject to arrest."

The letter was copied to the Lanesborough and Pittsfield police departments. Patricia signed it, but, for some reason, Neil hadn't. According to her statement later, Patricia never gave it to Christopher or sent it to the police.

Christopher found himself without a residence. Yet several of Patricia's employees later told police that Patricia allowed Christopher, without Neil's knowledge, to sleep at the restaurant if he didn't have a place to stay; and some later claimed she routinely gave her son money to rent a room at Mountain View. There were times, too, Christopher later admitted, when he dipped into the cash register at Mrs. O's.

When detectives arrived at the motel, Christopher was more than willing to accompany them to Pittsfield for questioning. Several things weren't adding up. For one, when detectives found out Christopher and Neil were at odds with each other, before they could write Christopher off as a suspect, they had to find out just how much animosity and hatred there was between them. Hatred was a definite motive for murder. Christopher had a baby with his girlfriend. He rarely took care of the child. But Patricia and Neil, a family member said, were thinking of allowing the mother of the child and the baby to move into the house. Christopher, however, wasn't welcome. Neil loved his step grandchild. He had never had children of his own, and to watch him with the baby, you would think it was his own.

But this, coupled with Neil's strong-arm disciplinary tactics earlier in Christopher's life, riled Patricia's son, made him very angry.

Was it, however, enough to turn Christopher from an irritated young kid—a dark, goalless, jobless, homeless roamer and druggie —into a cold-blooded murderer?

When detectives looked at Christopher standing in the doorway to his motel room, there appeared to be dried blood droplets and blood spatter on his pants.

Detectives looked at each other, then at Christopher.

At the MSP Detective Unit in Pittsfield, detectives read Christopher his rights and asked him about his life at home with Neil and his mother.

135

"Living with Neil was good," Christopher responded. Shabbily dressed, sporting a tar-black goatee, earrings, and tattoos, Christopher appeared raggedy. Friends said he used to be into what was known as the "Goth" movement, wearing black nail polish and face make-up to accentuate the look. There was definitely a sinister side to Christopher Robinson, at least one that spoke of his wild youth. Continuing, the boy added, "[Neil] always supplied us with what we needed, but I kinda grew up with the tough love kinda thing."

During high school, Christopher said, Amanda called Child Services one day and reported that Neil had hit them. When the social worker showed up to conduct an interview, Christopher explained, "I strongly believe in the family thing, [so] I lied [to them] and said nothing had happened. I didn't want to break up my mother's family."

Christopher claimed Patricia started "to have a nervous breakdown" somewhere around 2002. He gave no reason why, other than her problems with Crohn's disease. Regarding Neil, he said, "The last time I saw [him was] on Merrill Road. He was going to Home Depot. My mother told me they were rebuilding the house, so I guess he was going to buy stuff. . . . I didn't wave or anything. He saw me."

Christopher came across as fidgety, nervous. Something was bothering him. As he talked, detectives asked when he last saw his mother.

"Last night," Christopher said, "because I heard what happened and I wanted to see if she was all right."

After being asked, he then talked about what he did on the night Neil was murdered and the following day. At one point, Christopher said he went down to Mrs. O's. The feeling he got when he walked in was that something terrible had happened. "They were looking all glum."

"Smile," Christopher told Rosa and Casey Nicola, hoping, he claimed, to cheer them up.

"Neil's dead!"

"You're fucking kidding me," Christopher said.

"Hannah crushed his head."

Next, Christopher explained what he did the remainder of that day.

Then detectives asked: "Did you have anything to do with Neil Olsen's murder?"

"I had nothing to do with Neil's death," Christopher said defiantly. "We would get into a fight, but I would disappear until he cooled off. Then we would get along again. . . . The only thing I know about how Neil died is that Hannah stomped on his head. I've known her and she is old. . . . All I know is what they told me about Hannah and how they found him."

They cut Christopher loose. But later that same day, at 4:10 p.m., detectives caught up with him again. Christopher was even more disheveled and jumpy. He claimed to have more information he wanted to include in his original statement. Investigators knew he had lied to them earlier. After a quick look around as Christopher was being led to a patrol car, detectives had seen blood all over Christopher's motel room, in his car, all over his clothes.

"Come on, Chris," said one of the detectives, encouraging him to 'fess up.

Christopher looked around the tiny interrogation room. "Okay," he said just like that, without any argument. Then, without warning or fanfare, Christopher Robinson proceeded to explain what had happened.

He said he took $50 from the restaurant cash drawer, got a motel room on Sunday evening, and left his room at about 10:30 p.m.

"I drove up to Skyline" (the golf course next to Neil's house).

He parked his car at the top of the driveway, on the edge of the golf course. He walked across the driving range and hopped the fence near the horse field.

Then he snuck into Hannah's stall.

"I went in through the open garage door [and] stood by the second door. . . . I waited until I heard the breezeway door open." That sound was Neil coming into the barn to feed Hannah. "I put the butt of the gun on my right shoulder and waited to hear the door open. Then I heard the door open and I closed my eyes and pulled. . . . He couldn't see me because it was dark back there but he was looking right at me. I heard a loud bang and then a thud and then I came to and I was walking toward the black truck and down the hill. That truck is Neil's truck. All I remember is pulling the trigger once."

Pressing further, detectives learned Christopher "bought the rifle at a Wal-Mart in New York more than a couple of months ago."

For the next hour or more, Christopher described the events leading up to (and shortly after) Neil's murder. In pointed detail, he remembered times and places, even the exact amount of money— "I thought I must have got it from Neil"—he had taken from Neil's pocket: $186. But he continued to tell detectives he had "blacked out"—"I do that sometimes"—for much of the night. He couldn't recall, for example, going into Neil's pocket and taking the cash; but said he must have, because he didn't know where else the money could have come from. Then, "at twelve o'clock . . . [on] Monday, I called my mom. . . . She said that she thought I should get out of here and leave. She assumed that I had done it. I didn't say anything about that. That was it. I said, 'I'll just talk to you later.'"

Since Christopher had indicated his mother knew he had murdered Neil, detectives were curious: Was Patricia simply trying to protect her son; or was she saying, in not so many words, she was relieved her son had finally done the job?

"When I went to the garage [to kill Neil]," Christopher said, "I went there because I wanted to help protect my mother. . . . I was first asked about it after my daughter was born, so it would have been towards the end of May [2004]. My mother was saying how she was so upset and wished that things were better and that she wishes me and my sister were back in her life. . . . He wasn't violent with her until recently. She never really told me that he hit her, but she portrayed it as if it happened. This last time, beginning on Friday afternoon, he did hit her repeatedly on the back of the head. She told me this."

After claiming that his mother was the mastermind behind Neil's murder, Christopher Robinson went on to describe how he had tried to murder Neil on numerous occasions, but couldn't muster the "nerve" or "courage" to go through with it. He claimed his mother kept pushing him to get it done. But he continually backed out. He painted quite a picture of mind manipulation on Patricia's part, saying that, over a period of months, she convinced him that Neil was a brutish, abusive husband, and once he was gone, Christopher claimed, his mother promised that Amanda, Christopher, and his child could live happily ever after in Neil's house with her.

Interestingly enough, after describing a conversation he had with his mother about the bloody metal pipe found the day after Neil's murder, Christopher said, "My sister was there last night [when we talked]. She did not hear our conversation. She's kinda got a big mouth so my mother didn't want her to know."

According to Christopher, this manipulation by Patricia picked up serious steam during the summer of 2004. Christopher said he bought an eighteen-inch machete to chop wood and take on camping trips and then decided to use it to kill Neil. He waited outside the house several times, prepared to attack Neil from behind with the machete. But every time he felt he could go through with it, he backed down when the moment came. And when he failed to complete the job, he said his mother became angry and pressured him to go through with it.

But as January 9, 2005, came, Christopher said he had made up his mind. In a second statement, taken by Trooper Michael Hill, Christopher explained the night of the murder yet again, adding new details. He said he left his motel room around 10:30 p.m. and, a few minutes later, parked near the Skyline Country Club close to the driving range, which was separated from the Olsen house by a large culvert.

Quietly, Christopher said, he walked across the driving range, in through a small area of trees and brush, and made it into Neil's barn without anyone hearing or seeing him. Once inside, he found a cozy place by the entryway to hide, and waited for Neil to walk in. Hannah was outside the barn in her pen. Christopher knew Neil fed the horse every night at around eleven o'clock.

Neil Olsen was large man, big-boned, barrel-chested. Strong as rebar. He had worked with his hands all his life. Considering Christopher's small frame and frail body, Neil could have likely snapped Christopher in two with one hand tied behind his back. Hiding, ambushing Neil, Christopher knew, was the only way to get the job done. So, as soon as Neil walked into the barn and prepared Hannah for her nightly feeding, Christopher stepped out behind his stepfather and, standing about "a foot and a half away" with his "eyes closed," pulled the trigger.

After the first shot, Neil fell to the ground—but Christopher couldn't remember what happened next. He "blacked out." Still, the evidence proves he fired nine more rounds, seven of which ended up in Neil's head, and then beat Neil with a forty-inch metal pipe, hoping to cover up the crime. Moreover, Christopher said he left the barn door open so Hannah could find her way into the barn—and that he ran into his mother's house to hide the gun in a closet and explain to her what he had done. Both decisions would have taken calculated thought. It's hardly conceivable that he could have blacked out through it all. Killers—especially when extreme violence is present—have been known to describe a period during a murder as "hazy" or somewhat difficult to recall in full, much like a drunk trying to remember portions of a bender. Yet during those brief periods of blacking out, if you will, most killers don't remember much of anything, more or less just snapshots.

"Robinson stayed up until about four in the morning," Trooper Hill's report stated, detailing the hours following the murder, "because he couldn't get that sound out of his head. That thud sound, the sound of Neil Olsen getting shot in the head." Christopher said he felt "really dirty and took two showers and kept washing his hands" over and over.

The next day, apparently now over the guilt of having murdered Neil, Christopher went to the Berkshire Mall, saw a movie, *White Noise*, ate lunch at McDonald's, and even did some shopping. *White Noise*, a horror film about murdered people communicating from beyond the grave, seemed like a creepy, bizarre choice of films so early after murdering someone.

Asked why he committed the murder, Christopher told police he wanted to "help and protect his mother."

On top of all of the detail Christopher provided police during those two interviews a few days after the murder, he had even more to offer. Because in the coming weeks, Christopher Robinson would change his story yet again, offering additional, specific elements of murder that would further incriminate Neil's wife, Patricia Olsen.

~~~

Police had their man under a confession. Even better was that he had given up the crime's true motivator, Patricia. This did not mean, however, that she was guilty. Detectives had to build a case against the alleged Black Widow and, most importantly, try to back up what Christopher had told them. After all, without corroboration, Christopher's statement was nothing more than a mesh of words.

When detectives caught up with Amanda Robinson, it was clear that the young girl had fallen on hard times, but had also been trying to rebuild her life. It wasn't only alcohol and pot that had dragged Amanda down. According to Amanda's court testimony, she'd had a serious problem with cocaine, which Neil and Patricia had discovered a year before Neil was murdered.

Born on Valentine's Day 1986, Amanda was Patricia's youngest child. Quite stunning, with long blonde hair and, as one family member later admired, "puppy dog eyes," Amanda now appeared weathered and drawn. She was nineteen, but looked much older. When detectives found her, Amanda was living in New York with her boyfriend at his father's house.

Amanda admitted that, after she'd tried cocaine for the second time, in the bathroom of her mother's restaurant, she soon "developed more of a coke habit." Her favorite places to snort the drug, she said, were at home in her room, inside the restaurant, and outside in "the horse's stall."

As she explained to Trooper Jean Thibodeau and Sergeant David Bell, her drug dealer would come by the Olsen house and swap cocaine out for the money she left in the mailbox. She would wait anxiously, staring out her room window, facing the mailbox, and then run out and grab her drugs as soon as he dropped them off. This went on for quite some time.

"My mom usually slept upstairs," Amanda said, "and Neil would be passed out on the couch."

Working at Mrs. O's for her mother, Amanda said, was more of a chore than a job.

"I was working . . . like every night. I wasn't getting paid. I would go in my mom's wallet. She didn't call me on the money. I stopped getting coke . . . after my [last] birthday. I got caught by my mom." Patricia had walked into the restaurant one morning and threw a "rolled up dollar bill on the counter" in front of her, asking sternly, "What's that?" She didn't appear angry, though, Amanda remembered, just "disappointed."

"Why didn't you come to *me* about this?" Patricia wondered when Amanda didn't respond. Neil had found the coke, along with empty bottles of liquor Amanda said she used to come down off the coke. Neil knew it was coke, Patricia told her that day, because he had "tasted" the residue left in her room and it had made his lips "go numb."

"You need to get out of the house now," Patricia told her, "or you'll be grounded until you leave."

In her first statement to police, Amanda Robinson confirmed the telephone calls between her and Patricia on Sunday afternoon, down to the details Patricia had described during questioning. But Amanda remembered her mother calling back later that night (something Patricia had maybe chosen to forget) around 10:30 p.m.

She said her mother asked about her boyfriend, and then mentioned how Neil had been pulled over by the Lanesborough police because his truck was uninsured and unregistered.

"Oh, does he have to go to court for that?" Amanda asked.

"Yeah."

"That sucks."

Patricia said nothing else. They hung up.

A day or two later, Amanda couldn't recall exactly when, Patricia called back and they talked about what Christopher had apparently reported to police.

"Chris said that Neil hit me and that he was trying to protect me. Neil wouldn't do that," Patricia told her daughter.

In her statement, Amanda said, "She never told me that Neil hit her. She said *that* never happened."

For the next thirty minutes, Amanda told police stories about her life with Neil and her mother. How Neil's disciplinary tactics bothered her and Christopher, but yet, looking back, they were disobedient kids and perhaps deserved to be punished. She also described her mother's reaction to Neil's death as "distraught," saying Patricia was crying and drinking wine, blaming Hannah. "That fucking horse. That fucking horse."

By the end of the statement, one of two things became clear: Either Amanda and Patricia had gotten together and discussed what they would tell police (because their descriptions of that Sunday and the days following were just about identical), or they were both telling the truth to the best of their knowledge.

Concluding her statement, Amanda said, "My mom never said she didn't want Neil around. She mentioned to me a while ago that they argued, but it was nothing out of the ordinary. She never mentioned to me that she wanted to leave Neil or she wanted him to leave. She never mentioned that she wanted Chris to kill Neil. I don't know why Chris did it. Something had to happen to make him snap. That's *not* my brother. That's *not* the Chris I know that did that."

As police would soon find out, much of the information Amanda had given them in her original statement was, according to Amanda herself, spun into a very neat package of lies.

❧

It was the first homicide in Berkshire County in years. Christopher Robinson was arrested on January 11, 2005, for the murder of his stepfather, and was held on a $1 million bond, pending a later arraignment. Residents in and around Lanesborough were astonished by the news of Christopher's arrest, and more so by the gruesome details of the crime being released. Berkshire County is known for its remarkable aesthetics, fall foliage, breathtaking views of the Berkshire Mountains, the Norman Rockwell Museum, and the immense and sacred National Shrine of the Divine Mercy in nearby Stockbridge. Murder was perhaps the last thing on the minds of Berkshire residents as the 2005 holiday season wound down and everyone started looking toward the New Year.

When detectives returned to Patricia's house after interviewing Christopher, she gave them consent to search the house and, without so much as a breath, handed over Neil's dental and medical records. One of the detectives later said he felt Patricia didn't seem too concerned, and actually acted "sharp and direct" as they collected evidence. Patricia, whether she knew it or not, was on notice. Detectives were watching her every move.

"She was upset, not thinking straight," a family member later said. "They made a big deal out of what she was wearing on the night Neil was killed. Patricia couldn't remember. She called them pajamas one day and a nightgown the next—and *suddenly* that made her a suspect."

In all fairness to police, it was a hell of a lot more than a pair of pajamas.

Patricia's own son had sold her out.

At the foot of Patricia's property line, cops located the rifle Christopher had used to murder Neil. He told detectives he and Patricia put it in the house, in one of the closets, but he had gone back a day later and thrown it into the woods.

"They made a big deal out of Christopher saying that he went into the house after killing Neil," that same family member told me. "They claimed he hugged Patricia, and she helped him hide the gun in the house."

Why would Patricia, one might ask, hide the murder weapon inside her own house if she was involved? Furthermore, if Christopher hugged his mother, wouldn't her nightclothes be covered in fresh blood? Christopher had Neil's blood all over him. Wouldn't there have been blood in the house: on the doorknob, upstairs in the hallway, in the closet, the kitchen, anywhere Christopher had been *after* the murder?

Very little blood had been found in the Olsen house.

Claiming Patricia Olsen was involved in her husband's murder was one thing; proving it would turn out to be another matter entirely. Detectives would have to come up with a motive. Since Christopher's arrest, detectives had figured out that Patricia was the beneficiary of Neil's $75,000 life insurance policy, Neil's retirement savings, the home they shared together, and a half-dozen or so vehicles. With the enormous financial debt Patricia had run up between the two businesses, not to mention her total disregard for the household bills, state police felt they had a solid case against her. And Berkshire County District Attorney David Capeless knew he could easily explain to a jury why it was that Patricia wanted her husband dead: the oldest motive on record.

Neil Olsen was worth more dead than alive.

If Patricia seemed able to handle the stress of her husband's death as detectives and crime scene investigators combed through her house, it was only because she was hiding it pretty well. That would all end quickly. Three days after Neil's murder, on January 14, Patricia was admitted to the psych ward of the local hospital under observation (where she remained for several days).

According to detectives and David Capeless, Patricia hadn't just forgotten to pay the cable television bill for a few months, or simply blown off the light and phone bills, as most people short on cash do from time to time. Not even close.

By the first of the year 2005, Capeless said in court, Patricia had "more than $10,000 in utility bills and taxes . . . [and had] borrowed $45,000" from one of Neil's brothers "to prevent the bank from foreclosing on their home."

She and Neil were in deep financial trouble.

Patricia admitted becoming "sloppy" with their money throughout the years, but vehemently denounced allegations that she kept her inept bookkeeping and money handling skills from Neil. Instead, she and Neil were "extremely busy," mainly because they ran two businesses and didn't communicate all that well. Apparently, Patricia felt there just wasn't enough time in their busy lives to tell her husband that everything he had ever worked for during most of his adult life was about to be stripped from him because his wife hadn't paid their bills.

It just so happened that on January 7, 2005, two days before Neil was murdered, a police officer had pulled him over and ordered Neil's vehicle towed after figuring out that Neil had no insurance and no registration. As shocking as this was to Neil, a routine traffic stop had opened up a Pandora's box, police believed, of mounting financial debt, revealing it to Neil for the first time. Having found out that Patricia had failed to pay those bills, it wasn't such a stretch to think Neil went home and laid into his wife, demanding answers, probably asking to look at the household finances more closely. And once Patricia realized Neil was getting curious, it was only a matter of time before Neil would uncover the fact that she hadn't paid *any* of the bills.

By February 2, 2005, law enforcement believed they had enough evidence to arrest Patricia Olsen. At 12:05 p.m., police caught up with Amanda Robinson once again and confronted her with the notion that she knew more than she had admitted in her original statement. Amanda was brought to the state police barracks in New Scotland, New York, and asked if she was willing to add anything to her previous statement.

After discussing it with her boyfriend, Amanda told police she didn't need a lawyer. "I want to [talk] about my mother's involvement in Neil Olsen's death," she stated, understanding clearly that this was her one chance to come clean.

Amanda claimed her mother's obsession with having Neil murdered began as far back as her sophomore year in high school, quoting Patricia as saying, "Life would be so much better without him." Patricia was "evasive" at first, Amanda added, but soon came out with it: "Is there someone you know that would kill him?" she came out and asked Amanda one day. "I'll pay them."

Further, she explained how Patricia's desire to have Neil killed grew "aggressive." As the years passed, said a report of this interview, she would bring it up and "make [Amanda] feel bad about [her] life" with Neil, so Amanda would become comfortable with helping her "make all of her troubles go away."

Amanda said she "ran into Christopher" one day at Wal-Mart while he was purchasing a gun, which he eventually used in the murder. "He told me that my mom gave him the money to buy it."

Christopher couldn't recall having said this to Amanda.

During the last part of the interview, Amanda went into great detail about her mother's after-the-murder plan, describing how Patricia believed she was going to "get away" with the crime. "You're not going to get away with this," Amanda told her mother. "Yes, we are, as long as we stick together it will just come back to your brother," Patricia had said. "We should tell the police that Chris wasn't there." But after she thought about it, Patricia added, "They're going to catch him. But hell, it wouldn't be that bad a thing, because he would have a place to live. Do you think I did the right thing?"

"I'm a terrible liar, mother."

"Come on, you used to put on plays in high school."

"She thought it was a big fucking joke," Amanda admitted. "She'd fake crying and call Fred [Neil's brother], and I'd look at her [while she was on the phone] and she'd . . . turn around and smile at me."

During her arraignment on February 3, inside the Berkshire District Court, Patricia entered a plea of not guilty. Looking quite withdrawn, her dirty blonde hair wildly frayed and unwashed, she wept during most of the proceeding. She was dressed in a bright red prison jumpsuit, both her hands and legs shackled. Her appointed counsel, Pittsfield's Leonard Cohen, a rather well known trial attorney, and later, Lori Levinson, spoke on her behalf. Quite interestingly, several members of Neil's family were in court supporting Patricia. They couldn't believe what had happened. They felt they knew Patricia and that Christopher must have made up this terrible story about her to cut a deal with prosecutors.

Prosecutor David Capeless told the court that Patricia Olsen "cajoled and prodded her twenty-year-old son to kill her husband." Capeless was adamant about his conviction that Patricia was the mastermind. "She provided him [Christopher] with money to stay at motels nearby her house," Capeless explained. "Patricia Olsen provided [her son] with money, in fact, to purchase the rifle, which was ultimately used to murder Neil Olsen."

Cohen, meanwhile, reminded the judge that members of Neil's family were in the courtroom, and said, "I think that it's a factor the court should perhaps take into consideration—that the family of Mr. Neil Olsen, the victim in this case, would like to see her released."

Undeterred by the presence of Neil's mother, Ruth Olsen, the judge ordered Patricia held without bail.

The following day, Christopher Robinson was indicted and held without bail.

On February 9, Trooper Stephen Jones and Lieutenant Patricia Driscoll brought in the father of Amanda's boyfriend. Word was that he had spoken to Patricia on numerous occasions.

Amanda's boyfriend's father had run into some hard times recently, admitting in his statement he had been a "recovering drug addict . . . [who had fallen] off the wagon." He said he returned from Bike Week a while back only to find Amanda staying at his house. At that time, Christopher was also living there. "He owed my son a bunch of money, so I told my son to throw him out. I came home one day and found him packing a bunch of stuff."

When he saw Christopher, the father told him to put his stuff back into the house as collateral. Christopher could come and get the stuff as soon as he paid his debt. He even walked Christopher out to his car to be sure he didn't take anything with him.

"One of the things he had in his car," the father noticed, "was the gun . . . a .22 [caliber] rifle."

Christopher, thinking the guy was going to ask him for it, said, "Can I keep the gun?"

The father was a convicted felon. He couldn't have guns in the house. "Keep it," he said.

When police asked him about Patricia, he said she "upset Amanda a lot." He often saw Amanda crying after she'd had a conversation with her mother. On a few occasions, he had spoken to Patricia himself on the telephone. "She was kind of flirty with me on the phone." One time, Patricia said Neil "was abusive and beat [her]."

"Why don't you just leave him, then?" the father asked.

"I can't because of our businesses," Patricia responded.

The day before detectives questioned the boyfriend's dad, he said Amanda was in her room crying. So he asked what the problem was; he hated seeing her like that. Amanda was always so depressed. He knew it was Patricia causing it and felt helpless.

In a tearful reply, Amanda looked at him and said, "I think my mom pressured Chris into killing Neil."

"Well," the dad told her, "you should do whatever you can live with. If Patricia had something to do with it, then it did not seem fair to let Chris take the full brunt of it." According to Amanda's boyfriend's father, Christopher had severe "mental issues." But, at the same time, he claimed Christopher "seemed like a nice kid." Still, it was Patricia causing all the problems. "Amanda kind of hinted once that her mother wanted to find someone to get rid of her stepfather. . . . I got the impression her mother was looking for someone to kill [Neil]." When he spoke to Patricia himself, she gave him the impression she wanted Neil dead.

"Just the way she was talking about Neil," the dad told police. "That she could not get away from him and that she couldn't leave him."

Christopher seemed like the perfect hit man. "I can tell you that he was a little weird," the father said. "You could tell he was *out* there. The books he had: like black magic shit."

Under further questioning, Amanda later opened up about her mother's desire to have Neil murdered. There was one time at Mrs. O's, Amanda recalled, when she claimed her mom had asked if she "would either help kill Neil or find a gun. She wanted him killed with a gun," Amanda recalled. "She would tell us [Amanda and her friend] that [my friend] could do it and we would have anything we would ever want."

"No, mother!" Amanda said she snapped that day. "My friend is *not* going to kill anyone. I'm not going to help you."

"Well," Patricia answered, "can you at least help me get a gun?"

"No!"

Faced with growing evidence that she knew more than she had originally told police, on December 6, 2005, Amanda came forward and gave police a third statement. She now wanted to set the record straight. There was a phone call between Amanda and her imprisoned boyfriend, recorded by prison officials, which made it clear to law enforcement that Amanda knew even more. The phone call explained, in part, that Patricia may have been involved. During that call, which took place on the night of January 10, 2005, Amanda told her boyfriend, "That thing [went down] that my brother said, 'It was going to happen tonight,' and my mother said if it doesn't happen, 'She's gone.'"

Further, Amanda explained how "shocked" she was that the murder had actually taken place. She never thought they would go through with it. "I told [my boyfriend]," Amanda said after being confronted with the recorded call by police, "that my mother was asking me to find someone to murder Neil. . . . I can't give a timeline as to when my mom started talking about wanting to have Neil murdered. After a while, that became the main topic of my mom's conversations with me. . . . It's not that I wanted him dead like my mother did. I felt that I was being pressured by my mother to help her. My mother would talk to me about it morning, noon, and night. It wasn't easy living in that house. It was the only thing she seemed to want to talk about."

Someone close to Amanda, Christopher, and Patricia told me later that Amanda "lied about a lot of things" to protect herself from prosecution. That same source said Amanda denied her entire statement to police and "feels guilty" about it. The source said Amanda and Christopher had dredged up this terrible lie about Patricia to "get back at her" for the way Neil treated them. They were upset, this source was certain, because their mother allowed Neil's disciplinary tactics to incapacitate their lives and she never stood up for them.

Nevertheless, during the early part of 2005, days after her husband's murder, the pieces of a conspiracy to kill Neil Olsen fit together. The more police spoke to Amanda, the more she remembered—and the more those words made it appear that Patricia Olsen had not only sanctioned the murder of her husband, but financed, planned, and initiated it, as well.

State Trooper Jean Thibodeau said Patricia's "initial account of her activities the night before" Neil's murder "did not check out." Patricia had told Thibodeau, for example, that she went to bed after watching *Desperate Housewives* and the brief opening portion of the show *Boston Legal*. But Thibodeau soon discovered that Patricia recovered two voicemail messages on her cell phone on the night of January 9: the first at 11:56 p.m.; the second at 11:58 p.m. How could she be awake to retrieve those messages? And who would be calling at that time of night, anyway?

Christopher.

As detectives interviewed other sources close to Amanda and Christopher, people who could back up what the kids were saying, a rather sobering account of the last days of Neil Olsen's life came into focus.

During the months leading up to Neil's murder, Patricia racked up a litany of bills she couldn't pay. There was even word that, at one time, a foreclosure notice for Neil's house was going to appear in the local newspaper. Amanda said she started looking for a hired killer through her drug dealer, but realized after a time that her drug dealer wasn't as "connected" as he claimed, and the offer was subsequently taken off the table. But even after that, Patricia never let up, Amanda said. "I told my mother that I talked to a person about finding someone to kill Neil. She said she didn't want to know his name, but when I told her, she would say, 'Really!' as if she were excited the plan was moving forward once again."

Christopher visited his mother a short time before the murder and explained that he needed tires for his car. He had no money and refused to hold down a job.

So Patricia began funneling him cash.

When Christopher returned to New York later that afternoon, Amanda's boyfriend claimed he saw a box for a .22 caliber rifle in the backseat of Christopher's car. ("No gun, just the box.") So he asked Christopher where he got the money for the weapon.

"My mother gave me some money for new tires. I bought a gun and radar detector instead."

Amanda's boyfriend was on probation at the time. He told Christopher, "Get rid of the gun, or get out of the house."

"I'll put it in my trunk," Christopher said. Amanda's boyfriend asked him why he bought a gun to begin with.

"I am going to take target practice."

"That was his only explanation for owning the gun," Amanda's boyfriend recalled.

Before Christopher was asked to leave Amanda's boyfriend's father's house, he and Amanda's boyfriend had several discussions about Neil. Same as Amanda, Christopher hated Neil. But it seemed Christopher was confused about his association with his mother.

"I love my mom," Christopher said. Then, in another breath, "She's a manipulative bitch."

~ ❦ ~

The conversation took place over the telephone. Amanda's boyfriend was standing by Amanda as she and Patricia talked.

"I want Neil dead," Patricia told Amanda, "and [I'll] pay money to see it happen."

From that first moment Patricia mentioned a desire to have Neil killed, Amanda went to her boyfriend and told him about it. She grew tired and worried. She didn't want any part of it, she claimed. "I don't want to hear this," Amanda said after she got off the telephone. "I don't want anything to do with it." Amanda cried. It bothered her. "That's all she talks about," Amanda said one night. "She's so [screwed] up in the head."

It bothered Amanda so much, she once contemplated suicide. Soon, she stopped talking to her mother altogether.

"Leave him, mother," Amanda yelled over the telephone.

"I can't do that," Patricia said. "I'd be broke."

"Wouldn't that be better?"

"No!"

The last time they spoke about Neil's murder over the telephone, Patricia told her daughter: "I am going to kill myself right now." The reason for suicide, she claimed, was that no one would help her. She was upset the kids couldn't find someone to do the job on Neil.

Amanda started crying. "I do not want to talk to you anymore." She hung up.

It was at that time when Patricia, according to Amanda, started "working on" Christopher.

<hr>

After several days, about eighteen months after Neil's murder, Patricia Olsen—who had been telling friends, relatives, and Neil's family that all she wanted was her day in court to explain the truth—finally got that chance. On May 3, 2006, David Capeless began presenting witnesses in what was presumed to be a month-long trial.

But it was Patricia Olsen's defense that had their work cut out for them. In theory, they had to prove the state's case was built on liars: two kids looking to get back at a mother they felt had abandoned them. After a strong case presented by the prosecution, by May 18, Patricia's lawyers called Lynn Reilly, an employee at Smith Barney, a financial consulting firm, who tried to explain Patricia's financial situation. Then, later that day, Patricia took the stand.

Here she was, prepared to step up and defend herself. How dare these children cut her throat? A jury shouldn't believe any of it.

Patricia had gained some weight while in jail. She looked ten years older. Nervous. Shaky. Totally disheveled. An outright wreck.

For the most part, Patricia's direct testimony focused on her love for Neil and their relationship over the past decade. At one point, she said the relationship between Neil and Christopher was volatile: "I didn't believe it. I mean, I knew they hated each other, but I wouldn't imagine Chris doing this."

Finding Neil dead was the worst thing she had ever experienced, Patricia intimated. "I thought he had fallen. I really thought he had a heart attack, just that something was wrong."

David Capeless felt differently, of course. When he got a crack at Patricia, the elected attorney never let up, centering most of his questioning on the financial debt into which she had sunk the family during 2004. It all sounded good on paper. Classic black widow behavior. Patricia claimed she never "kept" their finances from Neil. She said they were "extremely busy" with both businesses and that the subject rarely came up—that it didn't seem like a big deal to her or them.

Money—of lack thereof, actually—was a motive for murder, at least from where David Capeless argued. Thus, he made a point to let jurors know that Patricia failed to pay more than $10,000 in utility bills and taxes, along with a reported $45,000 she borrowed from Neil's brother to stop the bank from foreclosing on their home. These were extremely important factors, and certainly proved that a motive for murder existed.

For hours, Capeless hammered his points at the defendant, saying once, "Neil was going to find out that *you* had disrespected him—and *that* would have enraged him, wouldn't it have, Mrs. Olsen?"

"You're wrong, Mr. Capeless. You are absolutely wrong," Patricia denied.

Regarding the explanation for running into the barn only to find Neil dead after touching his leg and seeing "flashes," as she put it, of Hannah and the horse's grain bucket, Capeless didn't buy any of it. So he decided to show Patricia—and the jury—what she claimed she had already seen: The murder scene via autopsy photographs. Capeless insinuated that there was no reason for her to go into the barn in the first place, simply because she knew damn well her son had murdered Neil the previous night. The fact that there was no blood found on Patricia's person indicated clearly that she never went into the barn.

"You don't want to visualize it, do you, Mrs. Olsen?" Capeless asked.

Patricia pleaded with the prosecutor not to show her the photographs of the graphic crime scene.

"You don't want to see what you never saw because you were never there, were you, Mrs. Olsen?"

"You're lying," she lashed out, "it's *not* true. I *didn't* want Neil to be dead."

"You knew clearly what was in that barn stall that morning, didn't you?"

"No, I *didn't*."

After several more questions, Capeless concluded his questioning.

Shocking nearly everyone in the courtroom, after Patricia stepped down from the witness stand, co-counsel Lori Levinson and her partner, Leonard Cohen, rested their case. Apparently, Levinson and Cohen believed the state had not done its job and the jury would see through what they believed to be a transparent case of two liars (Patricia's own children) trying to frame their mother.

❧

On May 23, 2006, twelve jurors and four alternates began deliberations. The jury must have paid close attention to the case as it was tried, because within a day they were able to find Patricia guilty of, believe it or not, first-degree murder.

Patricia looked on in total disbelief as Lori Levinson cried.

What had gone wrong? How could a jury find a woman guilty of first-degree murder on the testimony of an admitted murderer, his disgruntled, formerly drug-using sister, and her convict boyfriend?

Immediately after she was found guilty, Patricia was sentenced to serve life at the Massachusetts Correctional Institution (for women) in Framingham, Massachusetts.

In June 2006, Christopher Robinson pleaded guilty to second-degree murder. Yes, the man who fired seven gunshots into Neil Olsen's head, beat him to a pulp with a metal pipe, stole his money, went to see a movie, and shopped at the local mall afterward, this criminal had managed to get the Berkshire County District Attorney's office to agree that a second-degree murder charge was a clean swap for his testimony against his mother.

Some argued that Christopher cut a sweet deal, while David Capeless defended his position, saying he offered Christopher no such thing.

Regardless, Christopher was given a life sentence—which, by Massachusetts standards for second-degree murder, entitled him to a coveted spot in front of the parole board within fifteen years.

Patricia Olsen awaits word on her appeals in prison.

CHAPTER 8

Murder on Big Bird's Estate

March 2008: Woodstock, Connecticut

At 7:36 p.m. on Monday, December 12, 2005, the Connecticut State Police (CSP) in Danielson (Troop D) received a telephone call that seemed completely out of character for the area of the state in which it originated. For one, Monday nights, especially during the winter months, were not the most active time of the week for criminals. Sure, maybe a break-in, a domestic dispute, drunk driver, or barroom brawl.

But this . . . well, this was quite different.

The call was from a man named Jon Baker. He wanted to report that his wife, forty-four-year-old Judith Nilan, was missing. Judy had left their home in North Woodstock, Connecticut, at about 4:30 p.m. that afternoon for what Jon described as her "daily run," but had failed to return home some three hours later. It was unlike Judy to be gone so long. It was as dark as ink out on the streets of Woodstock, where streetlights were as hard to come by as office space or a corporate chain restaurant or retail store. There's no way Judy would be out running at this hour of the night. Jon was worried.

In talking to the police, Jon said he had driven the normal route Judy had taken during her jog. He knew it by heart. Still, driving slowly up and down those roads, Jon said, he saw nothing. "We'll send out a few troopers," the cop said nonchalantly.

This was the beginning of a nightmare for Jon Baker.

◄━━►

It's the cozy idleness of Woodstock—Connecticut's second larg-est town by area—that makes it so likeable and pleasant to pass through. The rolling hills of what seem like dark green carpet dur-ing spring and summer juxtapose nicely with what become during winter fresh blankets of snow that appear so pure and perfect you have to wonder if you're not standing inside a snow globe.

The roads of Woodstock are twisting and winding. There are general and hardware stores, cafes, taverns, pizza parlors, and even a winery or two. People smile at one another and wave. The 7,800 residents here go about their daily business and head home at night to settle into the privacy they cherish so much, snuggled up alongside a sense of security living in a remote piece of suburban bliss on the border of Massachusetts.

Woodstock is a town not famous for much, but ask anyone in Connecticut about Woodstock and you'll likely hear about the Woodstock Fair, which overtakes the center of town every fall. More than 150 years old, the fair, according to the Agriculture Society, is "a harvest celebration . . . a homecoming: It's fun, educational, and entertaining . . . an Institution of its very own."

Up on a rise, heading toward the center of Pomfret, one of Woodstock's neighboring towns, on Route 169, the Woodstock Mid-dle School sits near a town green dotted with century-old homes, antique shops, and oak trees older than the town itself. Jon Baker's wife, Judy Nilan, had worked at the middle school for many years. Judy was a social worker, one of those adults whom students admired.

"She was always so happy," one student wrote in an essay about Judy, "she made everyone else happy."

The middle school once received a stipend from the town to fund a program that was eventually tagged PEERS (Prevention

& Education for Early Resistance of Substance Use). Teachers, of course, wanted to do everything they could to promote sobriety, instructing kids on the dangers of making such unhealthy, life-changing choices as using drugs and alcohol. As the program was integrated into the curriculum, it seemed to be working. Judy Nilan, who had seen the effects of drugs and booze on students on a firsthand basis, later told a newspaper reporter, "I found it to be extremely successful because it focuses on the substances that adolescents are most likely to use: alcohol, tobacco, marijuana, and inhalants."

To Judy, these kids she interacted with every day were everything: her life, her enjoyment, her quest.

⌐⌐⌐

State Trooper Gregory Trahan arrived at Jon Baker and Judy Nilan's home in North Woodstock on the night of December 12, 2005, shortly after Jon called 911 to report that Judy had gone out for a run and seemingly disappeared. English Neighborhood Road, where Judy and Jon shared their home, is exactly what the name implies: a winding, curvy rural road that connects to Brickyard Road North toward the east and Rawson Road heading west. There's an inkblot of a pond not too far from Jon and Judy's country home.

Jon Baker said he last spoke to Judy at 3:00 p.m. "I believe she went for a run on area roads near our home."

"What was she wearing?" Trahan asked.

Jon said, "Yellow-colored windbreaker with a reflective stripe, dark-colored spandex type pants, black-colored fleece type gloves, gray or white sneakers, and ear warmers."

Those were great, exact details.

With that, the CSP opened an official missing persons investigation. They searched the immediate area around Jon and Judy's house first. Maybe Judy had gone out in the back, slipped on the snow, hit her head, and for all anybody knew, she was passed out somewhere, freezing to death in a snow bank.

English Neighborhood Road and the surrounding region are desolate and thickly wooded. Think forest. Lots of it.

Judy Nilan could be anywhere.

Meanwhile, as additional troopers arrived on scene, they retraced the route Judy had usually taken on her run. At first, troopers didn't find much and frustration mounted.

Where in the heck could she have gone?

Jon knew his wife. According to what he later said, they'd had a storybook marriage for twenty years. They spent all of their free time together: working on their home, raising a few dogs, bringing up Jon's children. They had been talking lately about opening their own business, a day care. Jon had spent time working in the business world. He knew it well. What could be better than spending the latter days of your life with the woman you love, working together?

Still, Jon needed to answer some questions. He was the last person to talk to Judy. He had reported her missing. *Was it all part of a ruse?* cops needed to consider. The most common suspect in any missing persons case involving a spouse is the other spouse.

As the night progressed, the state police brought in the K-9 team and the blue and gold Trooper-1 helicopter, along with additional manpower to assist in the search. It was getting colder as the night sky darkened. By midnight temps were set to fall into the teens. Then single digits. What if Judy had tripped, hurt her ankle, and was lying in a ditch somewhere?

Someone needed to find Judy before she froze to death.

❦

Judy Nilan had an insatiable appetite for sports. She loved being outdoors, riding her bike, running, or just working around the house. "Judy was a champion body builder," Jon later said, "long distance cyclist, runner, wonderful cook, avid gardener, and enthusiastically jumped into designing and building with her own hands."

Jon and Judy had purchased their Woodstock property when it was, according to Jon, "a shell of a home." Judy had never worked on a house before. But, like "most everything else she took on," Jon said, she grabbed a hammer and started banging drywall against the studs "as well as any contractor." All of it, insisted Jon, brought out a spirited shade of Judy's lovable character: In whatever she did, Judy Nilan gave 100 percent and wasn't afraid to take on new responsibilities. "I can't tell you," Jon added, "the number of times she would stand in the middle of our unfinished house and say, 'I love our home.'"

Beyond being a sounding board for students as a social worker, caring deeply about every kid she worked with at Woodstock Middle School, Judy was an exceptional mother to Jon's children. "It would be a mistake," Jon later wrote, "not to mention what a great mother Judy was . . . always there for the children and [she] never missed an academic, musical, or athletic event—and there were many over the years."

One aspect of Judy's life that the CSP did not yet know as they began searching for her was that Judy had recently been involved with the State's Attorney's Office in Danielson, working with state's attorney Patricia Froehlich in particular. There was a problem at the school, a sexual abuse case involving a child. Judy was a witness. She was helping the State's Attorney's Office build its case.

"I remember that discussion over the dinner table," Jon explained later, "and how furious Judy was at what had happened to the child." What inflamed Judy most, Jon said, was that "this child was somehow being blamed for what happened to her."

For Judy, here was "bureaucracy" at its highest level, at work. She had "no tolerance for abuse," or a system that the media portrayed as seeming to fail children over and over.

❧

On the night Judy went missing, a teletype went out to all the local police departments and other law enforcement agencies. It was sent from the CSP's Troop D Barracks:

The missing person is identified as JUDITH NILAN DOB: 6/7/61. She is described as a white female 5'2" 100 lbs, brown hair, brown eyes, last seen wearing brown ear warmers, yellow windbreaker with dark stripe, dark running pants, and white sneakers. Anyone who may have seen this female jogging in Woodstock about 4:30 p.m. on Monday 12/12/05 is asked to contact Connecticut State Police.

As 8:00 p.m. became 9:00 p.m., there was still no sign of Judy. An hour later, nothing.

It was as if she had run away, which Jon Baker knew could not have been the case. Something had happened. Judy would never be gone this long without calling, without telling someone where she was or what she was doing.

And then a clue—one very important piece of evidence that gave investigators a cold feeling that this missing persons case wasn't going to turn out the way everyone had hoped. At 10:25 p.m., Trooper Michael Robinson, doing a sweep of the neighborhood, searching the streets with a spotlight, came across a piece of clothing. As Robinson was traveling west on Redhead Hill Road—which connected English Neighborhood Road, where Judy and Jon lived, to Brickyard Road, in a semi-triangular-shaped tract of land—the trooper spied something off to the south side. It was a black and gray colored headband. Jon Baker had not reported that Judy was wearing a headband, but it wasn't too much to think that she had left the house wearing it. It was cold out. She had earmuffs on. The headband made sense. Moreover, the road where it was found was part of Judy's running path.

The headband wasn't what piqued the state police's interest the most, however. When Robinson got out of his cruiser and combed the immediate area near the headband, he found a receipt from a local sales and service store that sold heavy equipment and tools. Among the items on the receipt was a chainsaw. The date of the purchase: December 10, 2005.

Two days ago.

A man named Scott Deojay had signed for the receipt on the account of Carroll Spinney, who had an enormous estate up on Brickyard Road, not too far away.

Carroll Spinney is better known as Big Bird, the tall, yellow-feathered creature on Public Television's hit show *Sesame Street*. Spinney, a puppeteer, had played Big Bird for decades.

Even more than the headband and receipt, though, Trooper Robinson found something else. There were "several spots of [a] bloodlike substance" quite visible on the receipt.

Bad sign.

Upon further inspection, Robinson noted that "minute blood-like spots . . . [were] on the snow next to where" the headband and receipt had been located. What's more, the receipt, Robinson observed, had not showed any signs of "weathering."

Turning around, heading back to his cruiser, Robinson found yet another clue—which, added to everything else, made investigators assume something terribly violent had taken place on the road where these items had been uncovered.

∙──◆──∙

Seventy-two-year-old Caroll Spinney's estate is set back a ways from Brickyard Road. Looking at the property from the street, it's hard to comprehend how enormous are the house and the accompanying land.

"Nice grounds," said one man, "almost like a retreat with ponds."

The one image that comes through, however, as you stare into the property is that Big Bird cares about the landscape—and the gardening throughout is expensive and immaculate. Carroll Spinney was born in Waltham, Massachusetts, and made his name in show business as a puppeteer, mainly playing the roles of Big Bird and Oscar the Grouch on *Sesame Street,* an experience he once described humorously to a newspaper reporter as, "A lot like growing up to be Mickey Mouse—only taller."

The Spinney estate, which Big Bird shares with his wife and three children, is situated on a tract of land so far into North Woodstock that part of the property actually extends into Southbridge, Massachusetts. Scott Deojay, whose name was on the receipt the CSP had found, was a thirty-six-year-old convicted felon from Plainfield, Connecticut (about a forty-five-minute drive south of Woodstock). Deojay had been employed by Spinney for quite a while, and was a hard worker with a solid build. One man, who interviewed Deojay later, reported that he "was one of the best stone masons I have ever seen." Beyond building fountains and steps and patios, Deojay took care of Spinney's property and kept up with the pruning and weeding and grass cutting, or all those things a landscape caretaker might do. He kept to himself, for the most part, and did his work. Save for a few local merchants, no one in Woodstock knew Scott Deojay or could claim they had seen him around town. Deojay didn't live in town; he traveled into Woodstock each morning, worked, and generally left in the evening. During the week of December 12, when Judy Nilan went missing, the Spinneys were in Europe on vacation. Besides one other employee, Deojay was alone on the estate.

◆

Looking more closely around the area where he had parked his cruiser, CSP Trooper Michael Robinson noticed "skid marks" leading up to where he found the bloody receipt and blood droplets in the snow. After a quick measurement, he determined that the skid marks were forty feet long. They were definitive and fresh, just made on the road. Whatever happened had occurred within the past twenty-four hours, Robinson, an experienced accident investigator, knew for certain.

In such a densely populated area, with herds of deer and other animals wandering about freely, it wasn't out of the question to think that the person who had caused those skid marks could have come upon a deer and struck it. This would answer the blood question.

Still, the headband? How did it fit into a possible accident with an animal? Was it even Judy Nilan's?

By 11:33 p.m., the first witness came forward after police canvassed the neighborhood. A man said he had seen Judy earlier that day. The guy was a local who lived on English Neighborhood Road. He said between "4:20 and 4:30 p.m., while he was returning to his residence, traveling north on Redhead Hill Road . . . [he] saw a woman who he recognized as Judy Nilan jogging towards him heading south."

If Judy left her house and jogged south on English Neighborhood Road, she would have taken a *right* onto Redhead Hill Road, traveled a short distance west, then headed north up Brickyard Road, where she would have taken another right back onto English Neighborhood Road to complete the full circle of her run.

The neighbor told police, when they asked him how he could be certain it was Judy, that he and Judy "exchanged waves," adding, "She was wearing a yellow nylon type wind suit, black gloves, and possibly a black colored hat."

Moreover, off-duty CSP Trooper Todd Stevens, who was in the area of English Neighborhood Road that afternoon near 4:30 p.m., filed a report that corroborated the interview state police conducted with Judy's neighbor. Trooper Stevens was driving through the area around the same time. When he approached the intersection of English Neighborhood Road and Cherry Tree Corner, a road that led into the eastern part of Woodstock toward Route 169, a popular main road running through town, Stevens said he saw Judy Nilan. How did Stevens know it was Judy? Stevens had known Judy through "various professional contacts" he'd had with her throughout the years, so he recognized her.

And then another important clue—one that did not bode well for this investigation turning out on a high note. Trooper Stevens had noticed the same detail as the neighbor—that Judy was wearing some sort of headgear: "a dark colored hat or similar headgear," he reported, "a bright yellow windbreaker, and black running pants."

There seemed to be confirmation of that headband.

When Trooper Stevens passed Judy and continued north onto English Neighborhood Road, he saw something else. He later described it as a Ford Escort or Mercury Tracer, a station wagon, which had been traveling east, past him, heading in Judy's direction. The car was beat up, painted shabbily with a dull, black primer. A "white male," Stevens said, was driving the vehicle. There was no one else in the car with the man.

Thus, with the evidence the state police now had, it appeared Judy had taken a right onto Redhead Hill Road with this black car on her tail. What worried the CSP after gathering this information was that those skid marks and blood droplets, well, they were also on Redhead Hill Road, alongside a headband that, sadly, Jon confirmed later that night to be Judy's.

﹌

Connecticut State Police had a receipt with a few drops of blood on it. They had names: Carroll Spinney and Scott Deojay. They knew the name of the store from which the receipt had been generated. They had a headband. Two credible witnesses had seen Judy. Still, could they tie all of it, including that one small slip of paper containing blood, to Judy's disappearance? Sometimes the most obvious set of circumstances fails to add up to anything in the end. And yet, it all had to be checked out before the CSP could move further into another direction.

At 4:10 a.m., early in the morning following the night Judy disappeared, CSP detectives Michael Contre and Richard Bedard dragged the owner of the sales and service equipment center that had generated the bloody receipt out of bed. The man lived in Putnam, a solid thirty-minute drive from Woodstock.

The area of Redhead Hill Road where Judy's headband and the bloody receipt had been located was now considered a crime scene. It had been taped off. Investigators were sweeping the road and nearby woods for potential evidence.

"Carroll Spinney is a good customer," the owner of the sales and service center said, noting that the receipt was generated by Spinney's account.

They asked him about the name on the slip: Scott Deojay.

The man thought about it. "I recall Deojay and a heavyset female with blonde hair coming in on December 8." His records verified the visit by Deojay. "He wanted to purchase a chainsaw and bar oil and he wanted to put them on Carroll Spinney's account." The man said he asked Deojay who he was and how he had access to Spinney's account. Deojay said, "I'm the outside caretaker. I work for Spinney."

The guy wasn't buying Deojay's story; he told him not to let the door hit him in the ass on the way out.

Deojay became agitated. He said he needed the tool and oil to perform some work on Spinney's property. Then he became visibly angry. So, to calm him down, the female with him wrote a check for the items.

"You have that check?" one of the detectives asked.

The man said he did.

The woman was from Central Village, Connecticut, a small town outside Plainfield, Deojay's hometown.

"Did he ever return?" asked one of the detectives.

Deojay had indeed returned, just recently, a few days ago, on December 10. He bought a "splitting maul and several other items," the store owner recalled, looking at an invoice of the transaction. This time he was allowed to put the items on Spinney's account.

Detectives had a photograph of Scott Deojay. He was a rather plain-looking man with a thick, Tony Orlando/Saddam Hussein mustache that fell down below his lip line. He had the brown, beady eyes of a crow, a round face, and two days' worth of stubble. He appeared dirty and unkempt. He came across in the image as a loner—but maybe a gardener, too. It was clear from his darkly tanned complexion and crow's feet on the corners of his eyes that Deojay had worked many a day in the sun.

"That's him all right," said the owner of the store. "He was dressed in an orange rain type suit when he came in that day."

"Any idea what he was driving?"

"A small station wagon," said the owner of the store, "dark forest green in color."

The detectives looked at each other. They had a feeling where this was going.

~ ~

Few could claim they led a life like Judy Nilan's. Her smile alone was enough to make you feel comfortable and alive. Most of her family came from Oxford, Massachusetts: four brothers, two sisters. Judy had graduated in 1979 from Oxford High School. From there, she went on to attend college at the University of Connecticut, where she eventually earned her master's in social work. Judy's true passion in life was teaching and caring for children, which was evident in the way people talked about her and respected her chosen vocation. Her first love was her family. In 1979, Judy wrote what would become an endearing and timeless set of words family members took pleasure in later printing in the newspaper: "As the years pass by, we'll glance at faded photographs recalling memories shared with special friends and family, never wanting it to end. Memories are the only thing we are left with in the end."

Judy Nilan's adult life was dedicated to education. Woodstock Middle School once posted a tribute to her on its website, saying, in part, "Judy Nilan was a social worker at the Woodstock Middle School who had a tremendous impact on the lives of the people around her. Her positive energy influenced the students and staff in the middle school."

❦

The bloody receipt Trooper Michael Robinson found on Redhead Hill Road was a turning point in the investigation. It told investigators that something violent had occurred on that road. The question became: *Did it involve Judy Nilan?* Finding a headband near the receipt, a piece of clothing that was now also confirmed to be Judy's, certainly added to the gravity of the discovery, but it still only amounted to circumstantial evidence. In light of the evidence (and the name on that receipt), it seemed the state police needed to find Scott Deojay and have a few words with Big Bird's gardener.

Detective Marty Graham had been with the CSP for nearly two and a half decades. He had worked several of the state's most high-profile murder cases over the past twenty years. On the morning of December 13, 2007, Detective Graham and his partner, David Lamoureux, were called into the investigation.

"We were mobilized," Graham said, "to go up to Woodstock . . . and while en route, one of our guys found that receipt. We had an off-duty trooper who had seen her. We had several addresses for Mr. Deojay. It seemed he lived everywhere. We went to one address where he had lived with a woman who had three of his kids."

No one was home.

So they went to the next address on the list connected to Deojay. Again, no sign of their man.

Then they found Deojay's brother, who said, "I think he's living with this girl in Plainfield."

By now it was close to six in the morning. The sun was about to come up. A new day just dawning.

"So we knocked on the door," Graham recalled.

Deojay's girlfriend, a heavyset blonde, was half naked, still half asleep, when she answered the knock. "Give me a minute," the woman said before walking back into the bedroom to change.

Deojay was in bed. He spoke up when his girl walked back in: "Who is it?"

"The state police," the blonde answered.

Hearing that, buck naked Scott Deojay jumped out of bed and took off as fast as he could, not even stopping to get dressed.

◆~◆

As detectives tracked down Scott Deojay, several CSP troopers obtained maps and land records from the Town of Woodstock, as well as GPS readings they had taken themselves. It was important to get a clear picture of Big Bird's estate and its relation to Redhead Hill Road. Carroll Spinney's name was also on that receipt. It wasn't much of a lead, but checking out the Spinney property was certainly a starting point. Maybe more importantly, looking at all the information, knowing Deojay worked for Spinney, it wasn't a stretch to think that perhaps Scott Deojay had accidentally hit Judy with his vehicle. He might even have driven back to the Spinney property, located about 1.5 miles from the crime scene on Redhead

Hill Road; and if he had, the potential was there for evidence to be found on Big Bird's property.

Even though he was in another country, Carroll Spinney had no problem allowing the state police onto his property. The CSP had cleared Spinney entirely from any involvement. It was impossible, in fact, that he (or anyone living in his household) could have had anything to do with Judy's disappearance. They had all been on vacation at the time.

As the state police went through the Spinney estate, one of the troopers noticed something strange. There was an access road on the property, set off by an immaculate and immense stone archway, which led to a right-hand turn off the main driveway leading *into* the property—a fork in the road, if you will.

"We believe," one investigator later said, "Scott Deojay built the archway—he was *that* good at what he did."

The road led to the far west end (rear) of the property, heading toward a thickly settled wooded area. For investigators, it was a challenge just to get around the property without falling; the frozen snow on the grounds made the estate as slick as an ice skating rink.

Near the end of the access road was a picnic area with a large Chinese pagoda-like structure built up on posts in an A-frame. It had no ground flooring. Two paddleboats were stored underneath the structure. A pagoda is generally a term given to "a temple or sacred building, usually a pyramid-like tower and typically having upward-curving roofs over the individual stories," says dictionary. reference.com. It is a place to relax, sure. A structure separate from a main living space, where one can retreat and disconnect from the world. To the Chinese, a pagoda is a spiritual den—a temple, as its description clearly states, to contemplate those moments in life when one is trying to unite with a higher power or an inner peace.

What was strange about this particular access road was that there was also a trail of blood leading directly to the pagoda—and yet it stopped once you got inside, underneath the structure. The paddleboats, investigators noticed as they approached, had blood spatters and smudge marks on them. How could a trail of blood just stop abruptly?

It made no sense.

As the CSP continued to search the property, troopers looked up inside the pagoda and spied a set of pull-down stairs (as if leading to an attic), which were obviously connected to a storage area on the first built floor of the pagoda.

The blood trail had stopped directly underneath the pull-down stairs.

❦

Detective Marty Graham and his partner waited patiently at the door for Scott Deojay's girlfriend to fetch the gardener. They needed to speak to Deojay about the receipt stained with what appeared to be fresh blood droplets. It was too early for the lab to come back with a match, so there was no definitive answer as to whose blood was on the receipt or in the snow. Still, maybe Deojay could clear the matter up and point the state police's investigation in a different direction.

The key was in talking to him.

Deojay's girlfriend returned to the door and let Graham and Lamoureux in. "Where is he? We want to talk to him," Graham asked respectfully.

"In the bedroom," the blonde said. ("She was very helpful," Graham recalled later. "Ready and willing to help us.")

But Deojay had run from the bedroom into a garage attached to the house. His clothes were still sitting on a chair by the bed. He was naked as a jaybird and nowhere to be found.

"When we got into the bedroom," Graham explained, "we were all surprised because Deojay was no longer in bed, where his girlfriend [had] said he was."

"This is odd," the girlfriend said to Graham and his partner. "We were just sleeping. He asked me casually who was at the door."

After leaving the bedroom, realizing Deojay had bolted, Graham walked into the garage and looked around. Lamoureux went out to the cruiser to call for backup. With snow on the ground outside, Graham quickly determined that Deojay could not have taken off, or there would have been fresh footprints in the snow. Even so, Graham and his partner had to be careful on another level entirely. They were there, inside this house, without a warrant. All they wanted to do was talk to Big Bird's gardener, ask Scott Deojay a few questions and, with the right answers, be on their way. They weren't accusing Deojay of anything; they were simply trying to locate a missing person and the evidence had led them to him.

As they entered the garage a second time, Graham and Lamoureux heard some movement near one of the walls. The sounds were coming from, it seemed, *inside* the wall.

Scott Deojay, they soon figured out, was hiding *underneath* the house, in what Graham described later as a "three-foot-high crawlspace."

Graham and Lamoureux stripped off their coats so they could fit into the small crawlspace and have a look underneath the house.

"Hey," Graham said, his chest to the ground, "what are you doing?" He could barely see Deojay. Yet, shining a flashlight underneath, Graham could tell that "[Deojay] was bare-ass naked"—and also now shivering.

Even so, Deojay wouldn't respond.

Then a thought occurred to both detectives: *Why is this clown hiding if he didn't do anything?*

"Scott, we just want to *talk* to you," Graham said. Sizing up the situation, being well over six feet tall, Graham decided *he* wasn't going in to fetch Deojay.

Graham and Lamoureux were in a tough position. They had a woman who was still missing. With any luck, she was still alive. They needed any information Deojay could provide. The other side of it was: Did Deojay have a weapon? What was he planning to do? So, Graham said, he and Lamoureux, who was the smaller of the two troopers, decided Lamoureux would go in underneath the house after Big Bird's gardener.

That didn't work too well.

So they regrouped and decided, you know, why not flush Deojay out from underneath the house the old-school way?

By using pepper spray.

It helped that Deojay's girlfriend was standing there during the entire ordeal. In effect, she was the CSP's witness. They were still on "touchy ground," Graham explained later. "We weren't there to arrest Deojay; just question him."

"What's going on, Scott?" Graham asked. "Why didn't you come out? Why'd you run?" Deojay was rubbing his eyes, brushing himself off.

Deojay mumbled something about always "fleeing" from the cops. It was just habit, he said. He was scared. What did they want, anyway?

"Get him some clothes," Graham told Deojay's girlfriend.

Graham and Lamoureux never told Scott Deojay what they wanted to talk to him about after he pulled himself out from underneath the house. They asked him, however, if he was willing to go down to the local Plainfield Police Department and answer some questions.

Deojay, teary-eyed and shaken up from the pepper spray, said he had no problem with that request.

Strangely enough, Deojay never asked why they wanted to speak with him.

"We did the usual: timelines, history, trying to reason with Deojay," Graham said. "We were thinking that Judy Nilan was still alive and we needed to find her before she dies."

For example, maybe Deojay had hit her and panicked, so he hid her somewhere.

"I had no involvement with the missing woman," Deojay said immediately after the detectives asked him about Judy Nilan.

Graham asked about the bloody receipt. Deojay's name was on it. Why would blood be on a receipt he had signed?

Deojay said he frequently purchased items for the Spinney estate. He had no idea how the receipt ended up on that road, or how blood got on it.

"Where is she, Scott?" Graham took a stab.

"I *don't* know."

The interview went on for three hours. They got nowhere. "Obviously, our angle was, 'Where is she?'" Graham recalled. "We had nothing to hold him or arrest him on. We believed she might be alive. The interview went on and on and on . . . and we eventually got to the point where we let him go."

Graham and Lamoureux gave Deojay a ride home; he lived near the Plainfield PD. In the interim, however, they learned an important fact about Scott Deojay.

Deojay had been questioned about a rape in Plainfield years ago, which put a new spin on how he looked as a possible suspect in Judy Nilan's disappearance.

Once at Deojay's apartment, Graham and Lamoureux observed a 1997 Ford Escort station wagon parked in the driveway—the same type of vehicle reportedly seen heading toward Judy Nilan as she jogged past that off-duty trooper on the day of her disappearance. The vehicle in Deojay's driveway was black.

"This yours?" Graham asked.

Deojay nodded his head yes.

Graham and Lamoureux took a closer look at the car. As it turned out, it was registered to Scott Deojay's former girlfriend. Along the passenger-side rear door and quarter-panel was a smearing of an ample amount of blood, as well as a "pattern impression [of blood] on the rear passenger's side of the vehicle."

This alone was enough to seize the car pending the issuance of a search warrant.

They asked Deojay about the blood. He denied knowing anything about it.

Graham called in a tow truck and had the vehicle removed to Troop D.

"We interviewed his girlfriend, and she had a timeline for him going to work and coming home around his usual time, with nothing unusual about him from what she saw." Deojay, on the day Judy Nilan disappeared, had sat down with his girlfriend and her teenage daughter and ate dinner, the girlfriend said, and then he watched television and "did their usual stuff."

He wasn't acting unusual, she told Graham.

They interviewed the girlfriend's daughter to see if Deojay had ever assaulted her. They were looking to grab him on anything until they could find out what was going on.

She said he had never touched her.

<hr>

An ominous cloud of suspicion hovered over Scott Deojay. The CSP had his car, which had blood on it. They would soon find Judy Nilan's DNA inside Deojay's car, as well as blood matching Judy's type smeared liberally all over one side of it. As each hour passed, it appeared Scott Deojay knew where Judy Nilan was, and yet he refused to talk about it.

Deojay's girlfriend was not happy with the circumstances in which she now found herself. Here was Deojay at her house—a man she thought she knew—being accused of serious crimes. That morning, after police left, she approached Deojay, saying, "We need to talk."

Deojay knew what she wanted: *Get the hell out of my house.*

He looked at her, "I need ten minutes alone."

As Deojay went into the garage, his girlfriend followed him. "Leave me alone," he said. "I need some time."

So she went back into the apartment.

But when Deojay didn't return, his girlfriend walked into the garage to find out what was keeping him. When she entered, she saw Deojay standing with a "blue strap around his neck." The other end was attached to a rafter in the garage.

Scott Deojay was trying to hang himself.

She looked up at him and gasped.

"Say good-bye," Deojay said.

The woman ran toward Deojay and helped him down. Then she picked up the phone and called 911. When dispatch answered, she screamed, "I need help at [my apartment]."

As the girlfriend spoke to the dispatcher, Deojay kicked the phone out of her hand, screaming, "Give me that knife!" There was a knife on the tool bench. "I'm not going to stab myself," he pleaded, "I just want to cut myself down." The strap was still attached to his neck and the rafter.

Scared, the girlfriend reached over and handed Deojay the knife.

~

Back at Big Bird's estate, investigators who had located that bloody trail leading up to what they now believed were pull-down stairs heading into a storage room inside a pagoda-like structure, found something else.

At the edge of the pagoda, around the corner, was a wooden bench—another sacred place perhaps to sit and contemplate life's true meaning while staring out at the beauty of the landscape. In front of the bench was a "large area of blood-like substance."

Furthermore, on one of the "support posts of the pagoda near the wooden bench" was a second smearing of blood, which appeared to be tacky, fresh.

It seemed rather obvious that something terribly brutal had taken place in or around the pagoda. With those pieces of evidence in mind, troopers pulled the stairs down and proceeded to search the upper storage area.

As soon as the first trooper reached the top of the stairs, the reality of what had happened to Judy Nilan became sadly clear. There before him was "the deceased body of a white female . . . who was wearing a yellow windbreaker, gloves, black colored spandex type running pants, which were pulled down to her knees."

Judy Nilan was dead.

From studying the scene, detectives determined that Judy had been viciously murdered. This wasn't a case of a car accident gone horribly wrong. Looking at her body, the way in which it was positioned, investigators figured she had been "beaten about the head, her hands were tied behind her back and the rope was also wrapped around her neck and tied around her ankles . . . [with] black tape."

Judy's killer had hog-tied her.

"There appeared to be no rhyme or reason why her killer had tied her up the way he did," one investigator later noted.

In light of locating Judy Nilan's body, investigators asked themselves: If it had been an accident (if Judy had been accidentally struck by a car), and someone was trying conceal her body, why would he go to the trouble of tying her up and taping her body? The scene was horrific. There was blood all over the place.

"She was beaten really, *really* badly," one investigator said.

Another problem soon emerged within the investigation. GPS readings indicated that the pagoda was located so far from the main Spinney house that it was actually in another town, not to mention another state: Southbridge, Massachusetts. Thus, the

CSP were obligated, under the laws of jurisdiction, to hand Judy Nilan's body and the crime scene over to the Massachusetts State Police (MSP).

Looking at the evidence, it appeared Scott Deojay had struck Judy with his car—maybe even by accident—and then, trying to cover up *that* crime, hid her body. Then again, with the obvious signs of sexual assault and the circumstances surrounding how she was found with her pants pulled down to her knees, many investigators believed Deojay had stalked Judy for a period of time and carried out a plan to attack her.

"We don't believe," one detective said, "that Deojay struck her with any force with his car. There were tire marks left on the road. Sometimes, tire marks are tough to gauge. One theory was that Deojay knew [Judy's] route. Had seen her jogging before. Most people are creatures of habit. Could he have come racing up and locked up his brakes and stopped her on the road? . . . She probably stopped running and Deojay jumped out of his car and punched her because of the small amount of blood at the primary scene (Brickyard Road). He then would have somehow gotten her into his car. Now, remember, we later found a small amount of blood on the *rear* passenger's-side door of his car. When he gets her in the car, we believe, he drives her to the Spinney estate, where he knows no one is home because the Spinneys are away traveling. He then drives through the gate and the driveway splits. . . . There was an outbuilding: half bathroom-changing room and the other half storage. There were unknown stains there that came back to Deojay after DNA testing. One theory was that he assaulted or attempted to sexually assault her in this building and then brought her up to the bench that was under the pagoda and just beat her and then dragged her up those stairs. It looked like he just left her there for dead. Horrific. Truly upsetting."

Even though Deojay would ultimately never be charged with sexual assault against Judy Nilan, a source involved in the investigation later told me, "We knew that Miss Nilan was sexually assaulted. We found Mr. Deojay's DNA inside a [separate location] on the Spinney property. We also found his DNA on the rope he used to tie her up."

Judy's body was transported from the crime scene to the medical examiner's office in Boston where a complete autopsy was conducted. According to the ME, Judy Nilan died from "blunt force trauma to the head and neck." These injuries, said the report, "caused multiple fractures, subarachnoid hemorrhage, and brain contusion by manner of homicide."

~~~

Back in 2004, Scott Deojay had broken into a house in his hometown, Plainfield, and raped a woman. Because of Deojay's possible role in the death of Judy Nilan, he was nabbed for the 2004 rape, which had gone unsolved for two years. Addressing those new charges in court, State's Attorney Patricia Froehlich said, "This man is an incredible danger to the community."

Plainfield was best known at one time for its dog track off Interstate 395. It is a small town. The rape Deojay committed took place on the night of June 19, 2004, when a local woman was attacked in the safety of her home by an "armed man" who, after disabling the woman's telephone, "sexually assaulted" her, and then went through the house and took what he wanted. The description the woman gave Plainfield Police at the time fit Scott Deojay to a T.

Deojay had lived in the same neighborhood where the rape occurred. It was the type of neighborhood where doors were left unlocked. On the night of the rape, Plainfield Police set up roadblocks in the region and stopped people and asked questions to see if there was someone in town who knew about the crime.

It was that dogged gumshoe police work and the courage of the victim to come forward that finally led police to Scott Deojay. And when Judy Nilan turned up dead and DNA became part of that case, lab results matched the DNA from the Judy Nilan case with Scott Deojay for the rape and burglary in Plainfield. The system, you could say, worked in these two cases.

Scott Deojay was a repeat sexual offender who had graduated from rape and burglary to murder.

After his girlfriend talked him down from the strap in her garage, Deojay jumped inside her car. Meanwhile, the Plainfield Police Department had dispatched a few officers to the scene after receiving the 911 call from Deojay's girlfriend.

Deojay's girlfriend ran after him, grabbed the knife Deojay had dropped on the ground and, just before Deojay was about to pull out of the driveway, the courageous woman took the knife and slashed three of the four tires on her own car so he couldn't leave.

Deojay took off for another car in the same driveway, but didn't have the keys.

By then the Plainfield Police had pulled up.

❦

There was enough evidence to arrest Scott Deojay on suspicion of murder. Because the case originated in Woodstock, where Judy Nilan had been "kidnapped," it fell on State's Attorney Patricia Froehlich to prosecute Deojay, who was now being held on a $10,000 cash bond at the Plainfield Police Department, pending a court date at Windham County Superior Court the following morning, December 14, 2005.

Scott Deojay was transported to Day Kimball Hospital in Putnam for evaluation. Detectives David Lamoureux and Priscilla Vining showed up at Day Kimball to speak with Deojay. The state police had heard about his so-called suicide attempt and wanted to ask him about his possible role in Judy's death. In truth, they knew Deojay was involved. They just needed him to admit it. The evidence was outstanding.

The detectives read Deojay his Miranda rights. Deojay quickly declined speaking to a lawyer and signed a waiver, which allowed the state police to photograph several injuries he had on his hands and ask him questions.

Detective Vining, at Deojay's request, left the room. When she exited, Plainfield Police Department Sergeant Bart Ramos, who had been waiting with Deojay for the detectives to arrive, sat in on the interview. Detective Lamoureux began by letting Deojay know that they had found Judy's body on the Spinney property. Then Lamoureux said the state police were well aware that he had been working at the property as an employee of Carroll Spinney for some time. Yet as Lamoureux talked about the discovery of Judy's body, Deojay started to cry, folding into himself, weeping like an infant.

Lamoureux wondered if there was something Deojay wanted to talk about. What was it weighing on his conscience?

"While I was driving on Redhead Hill Road . . . I struck her," Deojay explained. He implied that he didn't mean to hit Judy. It just happened. "It was an accident. I believe she died at the scene."

Nonsense.

If that was true, the obvious question had to be: Why not call police and report the accident? Why try to cover up the crime? It's no secret that 95 percent of these types of hit-and-run accidents involve a driver leaving the scene, getting out of the location as fast as he or she can. It was almost unheard of that a hit-and-run driver would actually leave the scene *with* the victim's body.

"I panicked," Deojay said, trying to explain why he removed Judy's body from the scene.

Still, why was she hog-tied? What was the purpose of tying her up?

"I tried unsuccessfully to carry her up the folding ladder stair-case, after carrying her from my car to the pagoda," he said. Apparently, he couldn't get her up the stairs without tying her up. "So I went back to my car to retrieve a rope and tied it around her," adding that he used the rope to hoist Judy up the staircase.

It seemed awfully strange to Lamoureux that Deojay would go through all that trouble, tying the body in such a way, taping her up, placing the rope around her body—her neck!—in such a methodical manner, and then pull her pants down, simply to carry Judy up those stairs. Why not just dump her body in the woods somewhere nearby? Was Deojay to assume that no one in the Spinney household would ever go up into that pagoda storage area again?

Deojay couldn't give an answer.

"On the way out of the driveway," Deojay continued, "I found one of her shoes in my car and threw it behind a tree in the snow near the end of the driveway." (The sneaker was later recovered exactly where Deojay had said he tossed it.)

Deojay was released that night from the hospital and immediately arrested on kidnapping charges—the only crime the state police could prove at the moment—and held on $1 million bond. The medical examiner, it turned out, disagreed with Deojay's account of the injuries from which Judy Nilan had died, saying they were "inconsistent with being struck with a motor vehicle." Later, one of the investigators said, "I saw the woman. She was beaten severely. No way a vehicle did that. It's impossible."

On top of that, Judy's pants had been pulled down to her knees. Deojay's DNA had been found in two locations connected to Judy Nilan's body. His explanation that he had to drop her pants in order to tie her up and hoist her up the stairs made no sense.

The state's attorney's office believed Deojay stalked Judy Nilan, struck her down with his car, viciously beat her into submission, and continued to beat her until she died. It would be a tough case—especially on the family. Yet, as State's Attorney Patricia Froehlich later said, approaching the case was no different from any one of her other murder cases: "The same way I try to [prosecute] each of them, by looking at the scene, the evidence, the defendant's history, and by treating the victim's family with dignity and respect, which means being honest with them, whether it's good news or bad."

At first, it seemed like an ideal case for the death penalty. But Froehlich took a deep breath, studied the law, and realized it was going to be a tough sell. "As in each of the capital felonies I have handled," she added, "I agonized over whether or not the facts fit our very strictly limited death penalty law. There are two possible penalties for capital felony: life without the possibility of release or death. Our Supreme Court has very strictly interpreted our death penalty statute. The information from the experts, in this case the medical examiners who conducted the autopsy, led me to conclude that the facts did not fit our death penalty law."

In short, the medical examiner would have to agree that Judy Nilan went through a period of torture and extreme cruelty *while* she was alive.

Looking at Deojay, sizing him up, Froehlich later explained, "Scott Deojay committed at least two very violent crimes against women. He savagely murdered Judy Nilan and approximately two years earlier brutally and repeatedly sexually assaulted another woman in what was supposed to have been the privacy and safety of her own home. I can only characterize him as a serious threat to society . . . [but] I would rather not give any additional attention to a convicted murderer and rapist but would instead like to pay tribute to the memory of the courageous women he victimized."

As March 2007 came, with a little more than a year to think about it, Scott Deojay decided to plead his case out. After all, juries have little use for a two-time rapist. It would not have been a hard sell for State's Attorney Patricia Froehlich to prove that Deojay had raped, beaten, and murdered Judy Nilan.

During his sentencing on March 9, 2007, before a courtroom packed to capacity with friends and family of Judy Nilan, along with state troopers and police officers from all over Windham County, Deojay stood before the court looking disheveled and dirty. He wore a state-issued, banana-yellow jump suit, three days' worth of stubble, and a strange look of despair over his puffy face.

Deojay's defense attorney, Ramon Canning, addressed the court on Deojay's behalf, offering, for the first time, Deojay's "excuse" for the two rapes and murder he committed. In short, Canning suggested Deojay couldn't help himself. He had been wired when he was sixteen years old to become a rapist. It wasn't his fault.

Many in the room were taken aback. "What the heck is this guy getting at?" one person asked. "It was appalling."

Canning said it was the state of Connecticut's fault, essentially, that Scott Deojay had turned out the way he did.

What?

On probation as a teenager, Deojay had to visit Richard Straub, his probation officer. Deojay was now claiming that Straub had sexually assaulted him repeatedly for three years.

As Canning spoke, Judy Nilan's brother stood up and walked out of the room in tears.

In 1999, Richard Straub was convicted on more than thirty charges of sexual assault, kidnapping, and unlawful restraint involving sexual abuse allegations from more than a dozen of his clients. Of those victims, however, Scott Deojay had never been named and had never, before this day in court, claimed to be abused by Straub.

"The state had a great impact on him because of this probation officer's action," Canning explained. "It went on for *three* years and it lasted in his mind and caused an outpouring of rage."

The abuse excuse. How dramatic. How outrageous. How humiliating to the memory of Judy Nilan. Scott Deojay was a gutless coward looking for a way out of his animalistic, evil behavior.

"Previously undisclosed abuse is a tired, worn out excuse," Patricia Froehlich said, "that many people who finally face the consequences of their actions try to assert. I wouldn't have expected anything [less] from someone who committed the crimes to which he entered guilty pleas."

Superior Court Judge Antonio Robaina, clearly upset by the notion that Deojay had used such an underhanded tactic to try to lessen the impact of such a ghastly crime, explained that sexual abuse was no "excuse for these offenses. . . . These victims were so remote from the violence. [Judy Nilan] was a person who personified kindness and caring for others. She was clearly not in [your] circle of violence."

Picking up on that point, Judy's husband, Jon Baker, let it all out during his impact statement, saying, "Judy was clearly no victim. She was a strong woman who . . . accomplished more in her forty-four years than most others do in their lifetime."

When Jon Baker was nearly finished, he paused for a moment to collect himself before addressing Judy personally, saying, "Come on, kid. Let's go and leave what we can here. We have a future elsewhere—and maybe another song to sing together in the garden. I love you."

The gallery was in tears.

The judge piled on another twenty years for the sexual assault Deojay had committed in Plainfield, and sent Deojay on his way to a lifetime behind bars.*

---

* I do not want to sound as though I am in any way blaming Judy Nilan for what happened to her, but I want to say something here to any female reading this book. If you are a jogger or walker, I beg of you to take a different route each time you head out for a run, even if you change it up just a little bit. No matter where you live, no matter how safe you think you are, there could be a psychopath like Scott Deojay lurking in the shadows, watching you run or walk by his house or place of employment every single day, and as each day passes, he might become more and more obsessed with you to the point where he needs to act out on the twisted fantasies flowing through his mind. Don't give him that satisfaction. Take a different route. And also, please check the sex offender's registry in your area with a quick Google search and find out where the sex offenders in your neighborhood live. Believe me, no matter where you live, there are sex offenders near you. Again, I am in no way blaming Judy Nilan for what happened to her by saying this, but let us learn something from Judy's brutal murder.

A Few Final Words & Thanks

Reading this book, you might be inclined to think that murder in New England is a common occurrence, or that there is a certain violent component in the water here in the Northeast not found anywhere else in the United States. But the truth is these selected stories are the exception, not the rule. You are still more likely to be murdered by a family member or someone you know rather than a total stranger; and murder is actually such a rare occurrence that most will never encounter its ripple effect, as I call it. Crime rates are down in the Northeast and around the country as of this writing. This, mind you, while the reporting of crime and murder has gone up exponentially over the past ten years with the rise of the Internet and cable television.

This book has been interesting for me to write; suffice it to say that I generally write long-form books about one crime or murder. If you've enjoyed these types of short true stories and want more, write to this publisher and let them know. And if you have historical story ideas, please find me on the Internet (www.mwilliamphelps.com) and send me your suggestions.

Lastly, thank you for reading my book. I realize there are countless choices in bookstores today and I am grateful that you've given me your time and attention. I greatly appreciate you as a reader and am humbled by your choosing my book!

I'd like to thank Globe Pequot Press (GPP) Field Sales Rep Mark Carbray, who, in no small part, is responsible for this book. Mark suggested I write a book such as this and I took his advice. I appreciate Mark believing in me and making the suggestion. Equally, I'd like to thank everyone at Lyons Press and GPP, including Keith Wallman, my longtime editor, and Janice Goldklang, the executive director of editorial, Jessie Shiers, and Kristen Millett.

A huge thanks goes to my pal Gail J. Avino, circulation supervisor/interlibrary loan coordinator at Hall Memorial Library in Ellington, Connecticut, and all of the librarians at Hall who have supported me and helped me with my research, including Sue Phillips, Hall Memorial director. Likewise, thanks to everyone at St. Luke's Catholic Church (right across the street from the library) in Ellington, including my Wednesday morning coffee group.

I also want to send a special thanks to Lisa Sillito and Linda Pagliuco. Lisa suggested one of these stories and also helped with some of the research.

An immense thanks to Andrew "Fazz" Farrell, Anita Bezjak, Therese Hegarty, Geoff Fitzpatrick, and everyone else at Beyond Productions who have believed in me all these years, along with my *Dark Minds* crew: Colette "Coco" Sandstedt, Geoff Thomas, Peter Heap, Jared Transfield, Julie Haire, Elizabeth Daley, Jeremy Adair, Michael Dawes, James Knox, Nathan Brand, and everyone else who works on the show; along with my producers at Investigation Discovery: Jeanie Vink and Sucheta Sachdev. A special shout out to Henry Schleiff, president and general manager of ID, who has been behind my show since day one. You guys are some of the most professional and passionate people I have ever worked with. I am so lucky to have you on my side. I am grateful for everyone working on the series—you are all wonderful people, some of the most gracious I have *ever* worked with, on top of being new friends. I look forward to the road ahead and where we're going to take *Dark Minds!*

I would be negligent not to mention all the booksellers throughout New England and beyond—those indie stores and the chains—who have supported me and talked up my books to customers (thank you from the bottom of my heart); and my readers: you are the most wonderful people—thank you for sticking with me!

Lastly, my immediate family—Regina, April, Mathew Jr., and Jordon—who have stood behind me forever.

About the Author

Crime expert, lecturer, television personality, and investigative journalist M. William Phelps is the national bestselling, award-winning author of nineteen nonfiction books and star of the Investigation Discovery channel show *Dark Minds,* which debuted in early 2012. Winner of the 2008 New England Book Festival Award for *I'll Be Watching You,* Phelps has appeared on CBS's *Early Show,* truTV, The Discovery Channel, Fox News Channel, CN8, ABC's *Good Morning America,* The Learning Channel, Biography Channel, History Channel, *Montel Williams, Investigative Discovery, Geraldo At Large,* USA Radio Network, Catholic Radio, EWTN Radio, Ave Maria Radio, ABC News Radio, and Radio America, which calls him "the nation's leading authority on the mind of the female murderer." You might recognize Phelps as a featured and recurrent expert guest on the hit Investigation Discovery channel show *Deadly Women.* He's also written for the *Providence Journal, Hartford Courant,* and *New London Day,* and he has consulted for the Showtime cable television series *Dexter.* He lives in a small Connecticut farming community. Phelps can be reached on the web at www.mwilliamphelps.com.

Jane Doe No More

Also by M. William Phelps and available by September 2012, the true story of Donna Palumbo, a New England woman raped in her home by a masked assailant, whose struggle for justice was marked by a police department intent on discrediting her, the legal battles and media circus that ensued, her eventual vindication eleven years later, and her founding of Jane Doe No More—an organization dedicated to improving the way society responds to victims of sexual assault.

An excerpt from *Jane Doe No More* (September 2012, Hardcover, $24.95, 978-0-7627-7880-5) . . .

CHAPTER ONE

A Stranger in the House

The darkness swallowed her up that night. In some incorporeal way, however, it was that same total absence of light that saved her life.

The first sound thirty-six-year-old Donna Palomba could recall later was muffled and more squirrel-in-the-attic than anything obvious or particularly loud. Still, it was enough to startle her awake. Initially, she thought the sound may have come from a closet down the hall. We've all been there: jolted from a deep sleep by a sudden noise in the dead of night. You have no idea what the sound is, or where it's coming from. Donna couldn't establish what time it was with any accuracy, only that it had to be after midnight and well into the morning of September 11, 1993.

After collecting her thoughts, Donna was certain she heard footsteps: the squeaky creak of her wooden stairs heading up toward the second floor, where she and her children slept in separate rooms.

Those are not the tiny footsteps of children. . . . Donna considered. That noise, so distinct and frightening, was definitely not the innocent pitter-patter of a child rushing into her mother's room to snuggle after a bad dream. Quite the opposite, actually; this was positively an intruder's stride: heavy, obtrusive, stealthy.

The house was pitch-dark. Donna's fear—one of many, mind you—was magnified and made creepier by the stillness of the hour. Everything seems different late at night. More augmented and sustained. You hear things that aren't necessarily there. Your mind likes to play tricks, as if the internal filter between fear and reality, generally always there and alert, is still sleeping. As a woman alone in the house with her children, the crickets and late summer breeze outside the window the only sounds Donna was accustomed to, the last thing she wanted to hear were footsteps coming up the stairs toward her bedroom—and now it was too late to do anything about it.

Acclimating herself to the surroundings, Donna realized someone else was there in the house with her and the kids. And he was now coming around the front of her bed as fast as he could.

Donna hadn't been sleeping well to begin with. Her husband, John, was away for the weekend at a friend's wedding in Colorado. She would have gone with him had it not been for a business partner's wife, who was due to give birth that week. In one respect, it turned out to be a smart move: Donna spent a better part of September 10, that day, at the hospital, smiling, laughing, and holding the ten-pound newborn in her arms. What a wonderful moment and testimony to God's grace. Everyone was so happy. The talcum-fresh, clean smell and swollen redness of a newborn, gurgling and twisting her small balled-up fist in her mouth. How such natural, everyday miracles can bring so much joy to life.

Now this, merely hours later: a nightmare unfolding before Donna as she awoke to the sounds of footsteps. It was the first time in twelve years of marriage John and Donna had been apart. She was alone in a small community—the Overlook section of Waterbury, Connecticut, "Sin City"—inside a big house. Her five- and seven-year-old were sound asleep in their rooms down the same second-floor hallway. Donna had no weapon. No way to protect herself. No idea what to do.

It took a moment to register what was happening. She had been sleeping on her stomach, and did not have the opportunity to turn around before he was on her back, violently holding her down, the two of them struggling for position, man against woman. Not so much a fair fight.

The random thoughts, Donna explained, that pop into your head when you find yourself facing the will to survive baffle her to this day: *Blue jean material* ... During the struggle, she felt the scratchy crisscross patterned fabric of denim. She kept thinking: *He's wearing blue jeans. If you live through this, remember that.*

Some sort of mask concealed his identity, although she would not have been able to see him in the dark anyway.

Instinct and reaction took over. Donna screamed as loud as she could. Her window was open. Maybe a neighbor would hear and come running to her rescue.

Her attacker then buried his knee deeper into her back, reached around and put his gloved hand over her mouth. Donna could smell the fabric: greasy, synthetic, musty.

She bit down on his hand.

That set him off. He took one of her arms and cranked it around her back, wrenching it up toward the rear of her long, full and curly mane of auburn hair—as a bully might on the playground, snarling through clenched teeth, Say uncle and give—and held her down. Then he leaned over Donna's back and approached her ear. It would be the first of several times he threatened her life.

"If you don't cooperate, you are going to get hurt."

His voice was raspy. She first thought he had a Jamaican accent. Regardless, she believed him and knew then what he wanted.

If I scream again, my kids will wake up and find us ... Then what?

Obedience. Obey and live. Fight and die.

Donna's senses kicked in. She couldn't see, but she could certainly hear. This is how she would later recall the sexual assault—through a series of sounds and smells. Like a blind person, Donna began to see with her ears and nose. As he held her down, she felt a forceful tug on her nightshirt and panties, and then heard the fabric tearing as he cut both pieces of clothing with a knife. The ripping of the fabric was amplified and terrifying.

After he finished cutting Donna's clothing, she heard him reach into the drawer beside her bed, as if he knew where to look, and pull something out.

Then she heard a heavy clank: metal against wood.

In her mind, Donna Palomba saw her attacker placing a gun on the floor.

My husband John and I were married on October 10, 1981. It was one of those large Italian-Catholic weddings with bridesmaids, ushers, tuxedoes, limos, a simple, elegant gown made of satin in an off-white candlelight shade, along with all of the other amenities little girls dream about all their lives. I was a twenty-four-year-old college graduate from Southern Connecticut State University looking to start a family and a career in marketing. We lived in an apartment that first year. Then John found a house he'd had his eye on for a long time a mere block from where he had grown up in Overlook, a section of Waterbury named for its commanding view over the city. John's parents still lived there, as did his friends, cousins, several of his siblings. There was a pond a few blocks away where the kids played hockey during the winter months and fished during summer. Overlook was one of those Norman Rockwell-type of blue-collar neighborhoods centered on family, community, and God—a melting pot of many different nationalities, most with large families. My husband John knew and loved everyone. His mom used to say John was the only kid she knew with 300 close personal friends. Many were Italian-American Catholics to the core. The sort of devoted believers who went home to five-hour-long Sunday meals after Mass, mixing it up at a table full of relatives laughing, joking and arguing. In there somewhere was the traditional Ellis Island grandmother dressed in her tomato sauce-stained apron, talking to herself in Italian, scolding everyone with her rosary beads, crossing herself every time someone used the Lord's name in vain. A stereotype, sure, but also as genuine as the love they all shared.

The neighborhood was so tightknit that even as John and his buddies matured and went out into the world as adults, they kept their ties and got together any chance they could. The words family and friend meant something to these guys. They depended on one another. Everyone in Overlook seemed to carry on the traditions of the family business, be it insurance, roofing, construction, electrical, whatever. Your grandfather started the business, passed it down to your father, and you carried the torch until your son or daughter took over.

The fact that we had kids within the first few years of the marriage kindled our spirits; we enjoyed and adored being parents, same as our fathers and mothers had before us. Our kids would go to Catholic school, same as we had, and grow up being coddled, loved and cared for. Having kids was a gift I had waited for all my life, yet never realized or considered how much that experience was going to change and teach me about love and the will to survive.

Knowing her attacker had a gun, which he placed on the floor beside the bed so he could free himself up to rape her, sent Donna to an emotional place she had never been: a labyrinth of survival and mortality she had trouble finding her way through. She was now a mother protecting her kids, telling herself not to scream or make any racket whatsoever.

She thought: *I will give this man what he wants. God willing, I will walk away with my life.*

"As long as the children remained asleep," Donna recalled, "and I could convince him to leave afterwards, I felt I could come back.

I could heal. This man was going to rape me. There was nothing I could do to stop him. The only possible silver lining holding me together was the basic maternal instinct to protect my children and live through this for their sake."

Before he did anything else, Donna's attacker placed a pillowcase over her head, then he tied nylons over her eyes like a blindfold and bound her hands behind her back with the same material. She figured the nylons were the reason for his reaching into the dresser drawer next to the bed.

But how did he know where they were?

Tying her hands behind her back, he jammed his knee into Donna's spine and held her down. Donna could smell mechanic's grease and oil on him. Maybe it was tar, she considered, the same stuff they use on the roads. Regardless, these simple everyday smells were all-encompassing, stagnant in the balminess of the room. Later, those same seemingly ordinary odors would send Donna into traumatic spells of depression and anxiety whenever she came across them out in the world.

"Please, take anything you want," she pleaded. "My diamond is on the dresser. My pocketbook is in the closet. Take my money … please … please. Just *don't* hurt me."

With no response, he placed a pillowcase over her head; then tied another pair of nylons around her mouth. She was totally incapacitated at this point, bound like Houdini for one of his Chinese Water Torture Cell tricks. Only for Donna, there would be no escape.

The thought she had at that exact moment stung all of her senses: *How can I survive this? How am I going to convince this man that it is okay to rape me and leave without harming my children?*

For the next several minutes he sexually assaulted her.

When she believed he was finished, Donna spoke through the nylons covering her mouth. She realized later that "God had placed the words in her mind." Looking back, going through every moment of that night, she had no idea where they came from. Donna simply opened her mouth and the words were there: "Please … it's okay. This is between you and me. I will never tell anyone what happened here tonight. I don't know who you are. I know you're a good person. I sense that from you. I'm okay. I couldn't even identify you if I wanted to."

The power of words was all she had left.

From him, however, utter silence.

Her heart pounded with anxiety. Without warning, he placed the barrel of his gun up to Donna's mouth through the pillowcase. The steel was hard on her teeth. With the chamber of the pistol butted up against her lips, Donna and her attacker were at an impasse. This moment—when she believed he was going to fire that weapon into her mouth and blow the back of her head against the wall—made Donna's head burn as though it was on fire, a throbbing that grew as she waited for the end of her life.

I could feel the anticipation of death growing, a slow and agonizing approach. It was paralyzing. He was finished with what he had come for. He didn't need me any longer. I expected death to be quick and painless, though the fear of not knowing when made me shiver and sweat. This is it … I'm thirty-six years old and I am going to die. My kids are going to wake up and find my bloodied body on this bed.

I needed to prepare myself for death.

After he took the barrel of the gun out of Donna's mouth, she spoke: "Please, God, absolve me of all my sins." The words came out shaky and swift. Donna wanted to, but could not cross herself, as she would after walking into a Catholic church, dipping a finger in the holy water font.

Her attacker had other plans. Without warning, he placed the gun against her right temple.

Now he spoke: "If you call the pigs, I will come back here and *kill* you."

It was the first time Donna believed she might survive.

There was light.

Donna said later that at this point she realized she needed to "*will*" him down the stairs and out of her house. "That sounds crazy, I know," she later said. "But it had worked so far. I was disoriented, however. I had no idea where he was at any given moment. He was off the bed—that much I knew."

Still, something told her he was standing bedside, staring, that gun of his pointed at her head, now debating whether to pull the trigger or flee the scene. What could she say to this man who just raped and threatened to kill her that would comfort him enough to leave?

"Thank you. Thank you. Thank you for not hurting me," Donna said, not knowing once again where the words came from. "I promise I won't tell anyone."

She was certain the words sounded desperate and shallow.

The scariest period of silence of her life settled over the room. There were no sounds. Just silence and the subtle hum of the house pulsating and whisper of the New England night outside her open window.

As Donna considered her options, and maybe prepared for death, she heard something.

Footsteps.

This time they headed down the stairs.

Then the front door of her house whined open.

He's leaving, she thought.

An immense sense of gratitude washed over Donna. A moment before this, she believed death was her destiny. But she had survived.

The kids?

The front door shut. He was out of the house. Donna was overcome with a sense of relief, yes, but more than anything, gratitude.

This man had allowed me to live. This was all I needed. I could overcome the rape and heal. I had my life, which was enough to convince me that I had decades ahead of me to live. Just before this moment I didn't think I was going to have a life. What will I do with this life? I was transformed then and there. Every day, I knew, would be a gift I could no longer ignore.

Quickly, I broke free from the nylons, which tore apart but stayed on one of my hands like a wristband. I pulled the nylons covering my mouth down and let it slip onto my neck as though it was a handkerchief or scarf. Only then was I able to take the pillowcase off my head.

I ran down the hall to check on the kids.

They were both still sound asleep. I knelt down beside my daughter's bed as her bony chest moved slowly up and down as a metronome to the faint whistle coming from her nose. I dropped my head, closed my eyes, and sobbed.

I wondered if he was outside waiting to see what I was going to do. I needed to call for help.

Family, I thought. Call someone from the family … he told you not to call the police.

Donna went back to her bedroom and picked up the telephone. No dial tone.

So she rushed downstairs.

The phone line in the kitchen, same as the one upstairs in Donna's room—the only two phone lines in the house—was out of service.

In an age without cell phones, Donna was stuck inside her house with her kids, no way to communicate with the outside world, and no idea if her attacker was outside waiting for her to emerge.

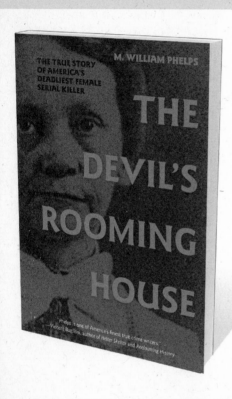
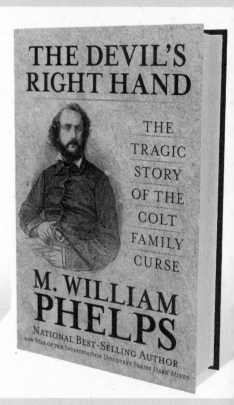
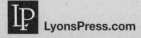